THEOLOGY OF THE PAIN OF GOD

Theology of the Pain of God

BY KAZOH KITAMORI

Wipf & Stock
PUBLISHERS
Eugene, Oregon

This book is a translation of *KAMI NO ITAMI NO SHINGAKU*, published by Shinkyo Shuppansha, Tokyo, Japan, © 1958 (5th Revised Edition).

Wipf and Stock Publishers
199 W 8th Ave, Suite 3
Eugene, OR 97401

Theology of the Pain of God
The First Original Theology From Japan
By Kitamori, Kazoh
Copyright©1965 by Kitamori, Kazoh
ISBN: 1-59752-256-2
Publication date 6/10/2005
Previously published by John Knox Press, 1965

FOREWORD

No Japanese theologian has had a broader international readership than Kazoh Kitamori (1916–98) did. First published in Japanese (1946), *The Theology of the Pain of God* has been translated into English (1965), German (1972), Spanish (1975), Italian (1975), and Korean (1987). It was a major subject of discussion for, among others, Carl Michalson (1960), Heinrich Ott (1966), Jürgen Moltmann (1972), Dorothe Sølle (1973), Hans Küng (1978), Rudolf Bohren (1980), and Alister McGrath (1994). The book bears the hallmark of Japanese theology's genuine originality, and has contributed much to the contemporary understanding of the Biblical God.

Readers will be surprised to know, however, that Kitamori was never a mainstream theologian in his native Japan. This book concludes with a quotation from Hebrews 13:12, "Jesus also suffered outside the gate." Despite his hopeful remarks in the Preface, the author and his work remained outside of Japanese theological circles. As a student who attended some of his last classes at Tokyo Union Theological Seminary, I admired his ability to spin complex Hegelian thoughts into perfectly organized and sometimes even memorable sentences. But what I saw outside the classroom was a rather solitary figure amid much international acclaim.

Professor Kitamori was a minority Lutheran by confession, and remained so even after his and other churches merged into the United Church of Christ in Japan (*Kyodan*) in 1941. He was also a vocal critic of Karl Barth, as is evident in this book, when most Japanese theologians were mesmerized by Barth's radical dialectics. One can also cite the persistent doubts about his patripassianism, which he clearly refutes in the following pages. These facts may have contributed to his alienation from the predominantly Reformed and staunchly orthodox seminary faculty. But more to the point, postwar Japanese theologians were utterly skeptical about their own cultural heritage. "Can anything good come out of Nazareth?" (John 1:46) This atmosphere among conscientious Christians is certainly understandable in the wake of the all-consuming World War II that inflicted unprecedented suffering upon millions. Relating the suffering of God to a Japanese traditional *Kabuki* drama must have sounded almost blasphemous to those who sincerely wanted Japan to overcome its unforgivable past.

Born in 1916 in Kyushu, Kitamori encountered the Lutheran ministry there and became Christian while he was still in high school. He went straight to a small Lutheran seminary, and after graduation he enrolled in the prestigious Kyoto Imperial University, whose faculty boasted a line of renowned philosophers such as Kitaro Nishida, Hajime Tanabe, Seiichi Hatano, and Tetsuro Watsuji. It is true that he completed this book at the very height of the war, but the central theme of the pain of God was fully developed by the time he graduated from the seminary in 1938, i.e., before he was schooled in the Kyoto philosophy. Kitamori then started teaching at Tokyo Union Theological Seminary and remained there until his retirement nearly forty years later in 1984. He was also a devoted minister of a local church in Tokyo, which he founded and pastored for forty-six years until 1996. A prolific writer of some forty books in Japanese, he was always accompanied by a group of dedicated followers wherever he lectured or preached. He never married.

Recent re-assessments of his theology of the cross have generated yet more criticism. Written during the war years, the book does refer to the tragic suffering of Japanese people as a medium through which one perceives the pain of God (see chapter 11). But nowhere in the book does the author mention the suffering of people in other Asian countries that endured Japanese aggression and invasion. It would be unrealistic to assume that ordinary Japanese citizens had any substantial knowledge of what was going on outside the country when news and reports were tightly controlled by the military regime, but it does give the impression that the "pain" to which Kitamori refers is little more than an abstract idea.

If he did not personally experience the pain at that time, he certainly must have subsequently. When the war was over, the government control of *Kyodan* loosened, and the church began to dissolve into former denominations. Kitamori, however, was a stalwart who firmly believed in the unity of the church. His theological and ecclesiastical stature often thrust him into the vanguard of controversy. He single-handedly supported the consolidation of the faltering church by drafting the confession of faith as the basis of its unification. I still remember his vivid recounting of the difficult battles he had to wage. His stories would invariably end with the phrase *"Athanasius contra mundum,"* with colorful anecdotes of how Athanasius fought to prevail over the Arian majority for the unifying confession of *"homoousious."* The result is a confession that is faithful to the apostolic tradition and yet broad enough to embrace a variety of denominations. In the ensuing years of student revolution, an agitated student slapped him across the face at a public meeting. He thus had to practice what he preached: forgiving the unforgivable and embracing what cannot be embraced.

As a native Japanese, I can only appreciate the effort of the translator and praise his excellent English rendition. There is, however, one footnote that I would like to add. At the heart of Kitamori's theology is his often-repeated phrase, "embrace those who should not be embraced." Careful readers will notice that this phrase has meanings that are more than ethical. The original Japanese (*bekarazaru*), translated here as "should not," may also be translated ontologically as "cannot." The pain of God arises because God embraces what "cannot" be embraced. God aches, because he is at pains to accept what "cannot" be accepted. God suffers, because he contains what "cannot" be contained.

I congratulate the decision of Wipf and Stock Publishers to reprint this monumental theological monograph and hope that in the days to come Japanese theologians will continue to contribute to the richness of the understanding of our Gospel.

Anri Morimoto
International Christian University, Tokyo
June 2005

CONTENTS

Preface to the English Edition 7
Preface to the Second Edition 9
Preface to the Third Edition 11
Preface to the Fourth Edition 13
Preface to the Fifth Edition 15
I God in Pain 19
II The Pain of God and the Historical Jesus 32
III Pain as the Essence of God 44
IV Service for the Pain of God 50
V The Symbol of the Pain of God 58
VI The Mysticism of Pain 71
VII The Pain of God and Ethics 85
VIII The Immanence and Transcendence of the Pain of God 98
IX The Pain of God and the Hidden God 105
X The Order of Love 117
XI The Pain of God and Gospel History 128
XII The Pain of God and Eschatology 139
XIII Conclusion 145
Appendix: Jeremiah 31:20 and Isaiah 63:15 151
Notes 169
Index of Names 179
Index of Scripture Passages 181

PREFACE TO THE ENGLISH EDITION

I believe this is the first strictly theological Japanese book to be introduced in the English-speaking world. Although the writings of Toyohiko Kagawa and Kanzo Uchimura have been translated into English, they are not theology in the strict sense of the word. This translation partly owes its appearance to Professor Carl Michalson's *Japanese Contributions to Christian Theology*, in which he says that my theology is "the most self-consciously Japanese of the current theological tendencies in Japan. Yet it seems the most likely to interest and appeal to the theologians of the West, especially to Americans."

Here I would like to mention the Japanese characteristics of this book and the relation of this theology to Western theology. The word "Japanese" can be included under the terms "Asian" or "non-Western." Previously, Christian theology was written almost completely in the West. Not until the twentieth century was Christian theology written in the non-Western world. Just as during a certain period of history a particular Christian theology was formulated, so a time has come for universal or ecumenical theology to appear.

However, on what grounds can Japanese theology, as non-Western theology, claim to be part of the history of Christian thought? Can it be simply because the Japanese variety is exotic, as compared to Western theology? Or can it be evidence of the maturity of the so-called younger churches? I believe neither of these reasons is primary. Rather, non-Western theology can claim its own unique contribution to the understanding of the gospel. Chapter Three, "Pain as the Essence of God," and Chapter Eleven, "The Pain of God and Gospel History," are written especially with this in mind. Ecumenical theology is concretely, not abstractly, universal. That is, it is the universal mediated by the particular. Thus, for example, Greek theology is a particular theology. Orthodox dogma, like ecumenical theology, was mediated by a particular theology, in this case, Greek theology. Greek theology can claim universal validity since it gave birth to orthodox dogma, but, it is still open to question, since it is a particular theology.

Although it may be difficult to raise this question in the West, it should not be surprising if non-Western theology challenges this aspect. It may be asked, On what grounds does non-Western theology raise questions about Greek (Western) theology? The answer is, Did this theology transmit the message of the gospel correctly? I feel that non-Western theology is more sensitive about this point than Western theology. Greek theology, seeking to transmit the message of the Bible, performed this function in its own way; however, precisely for this reason, it created problems. If this is correct, is it not legitimate for Japanese theology, as a non-Western theology freed from the particularity of Greek theology, to approach the Bible from a fresh point of view?

At the same time, this non-Western theology definitely must be mediated through Greek theology as theology of the West. To the extent it is mediated by the tradition of orthodox (Western) dogma, it tries to renew that tradition even as it seeks to approach the very message of the Bible.

I would like to add a word about the pain of God; in my theology it is used as a technical term. That is, it is used as an expression with a special content based on a premise. This phrase is taken from Jeremiah 31:20. I first discovered this phrase in the Japanese Literary Version; it can be translated "My heart is pained." Luther's translation, *"Darum bricht mir mein Herz"* ("Therefore my heart is broken"), comes closest to that rendering. The King James Version is similar: ". . . my bowels are troubled for him." Translations along this line have a scholarly basis, as shown in the Appendix. Unfortunately, recent versions have gradually abandoned this type of translation. Thus I feel obliged to use the phrase "pain of God" as a technical term to express my dissatisfaction with these later renderings. (The Preface to the Fifth Edition contains a more detailed discussion of this point.)

Kazoh Kitamori, *Tokyo*

PREFACE TO THE SECOND EDITION

The first edition of this book was published without a preface. I felt no need to write a preface at that time, since almost all I had to say was in the book itself. Now that a year has passed, I find the theological situation in Japan changed, and my attitude changed; thus it is necessary to write a preface.

In the conclusion of this book, I wrote that the theology of the pain of God must remain "outside the gate, outside the city." But today I find myself, with surprise and perplexity, watching the theology of the pain of God drawn "inside the gate, into the heart of the city." How could I have anticipated a year ago that the "theology of pain" would become a fashionable phrase? Under the circumstances, I must renew my determination to "go forth to him outside the camp, bearing abuse for him."

However, I have two contradictory feelings: one is an urge for an affectionate response to the brothers and sisters who have been bound together in love through this book; the other is an urge for praise of God's grace which should be continued throughout the book. Knowing that there are many readers who came to be joined, literally, in the fellowship of brothers and sisters, I earnestly pray that the purpose of this book may be accomplished more fully in response to this love. This is a contradictory feeling I encounter in my determination to go "outside the gate."

The latter feeling does not require further description. I continue to advocate the theme of this book, not to insist on my own viewpoint, but to praise God's grace. Who can stop our praise for grace? This urge for praise makes me pray that the purpose of the book may be accomplished more fully in our world. This is another contradictory feeling I encounter in my determination to go "outside the gate."

Only misprints were corrected in this edition. The section on "Jeremiah 31:20 and Isaiah 63:15," which appeared in my earlier work, *Theology and Creed*, was added as an appendix in response to many requests.

I wish to express my continued gratitude and appreciation to the staff of Shinkyo Shuppansha (Protestant Publishing Company).

K. K., *October* 1947

PREFACE TO THE THIRD EDITION

This book has gone through many experiences since its second printing. It is a new experience for the book to be circulated outside the churches. Philosophers and men of letters have shown an interest in the book. I had to listen to their comments intently, with surprise and bewilderment.

However, I listened to the comments of the Roman Catholics and the members of the Non-Church Movement with interest. Especially the book enjoyed a great experience in opening conversations with the members of the Non-Church Movement. Hitherto our Protestant churches and Non-Church Movement had engaged in a rather nonproductive conversation, which is now turning into productive conversation. It is a joy to learn that the book served this fruitful purpose.

Dr. Emil Brunner said to me just before his departure from Japan: "Your theology is opening up a new line." I had talked with Dr. Brunner on many occasions, but I had never initiated discussion on my theology with him. He must have heard about my theology elsewhere.

Of all the comments I received, I was most struck by one saying that this book has a practical significance. I must mention two things concerning this comment.

First, the primary theme of this book is to behold the pain of God, since the theology of the pain of God is literally concerned with *his* pain. Our *human* pain should only be considered as service to *God's* pain, even though our human pain may sometimes be discussed in terms of ethics in this book.

Second, the theology of the pain of God really aims at producing the practical actions of our own pain. The pain of God rejects all the present human situations, because of its conflicting nature in that God is in pain. Here the theology of the pain of God plays a significant role in producing positive moral actions through human existence. This truth was discussed rather implicitly in this book. My book *God and Man* deals with this matter more explicitly.

I must confess that my life was drawn into the practice of this truth during the past three years. This truth encounters the problem of a new "church formation" in Japan.* The "system" of the theology of the pain of God, if such exists, is the truth which "unites the divisions." Because the purpose of a *new* church formation was to unite the divisions, I was compelled to participate in this effort with this theology. One of the tasks of the theology of the pain of God was to suggest that such a "unity of divisions" cannot be based on idealism.

The divisions of the world are becoming sharper and sharper in recent years. The recklessly torn situations of World War II, during which time this book was written, appear to have become worse. We must deal with the situation pointblank. We must proclaim again, and in a most radical way, the straightforward theme of this book: "God embracing completely those who should not be embraced"—that is, "God in pain"!

All the efforts to bring peace in the world—"the unity of the divisions"—will be vain without being supported by a cornerstone, "God in pain." God who "embraces those who should not be embraced" alone can reconcile the world to himself (2 Cor. 5:18-20). The pain of God brings unity to the divisions existing between him and the world. The world at war is a world separated from God, even before it is a world divided against itself. In order to have true peace, the divisions between God and the world must be united, even before the divisions within the world are united. Only those who know the meaning of this true peace can pray and hope for the peace which will unite the divisions in the world. "To have hope" is the greatest Christian action in our days. The theology of the pain of God must have practical significance in this area, too.

K. K., *January 1951*

* Translator's note: This refers to the formation of the United Church of Christ in Japan, which continues to strive for theological and confessional unity among those former denominational churches.

PREFACE TO THE FOURTH EDITION

It has been a new experience for me to find, since its third printing, that this book was studied and understood by those overseas.

I have also experienced the message contained in this book ever deepening in my conviction:

First, it has increasingly become my conviction that the primary task of theology must be concerned with "substance" and "content" rather than with mere "system" of thought. (See pages 28-29, 58, of this book.) The splendor of the content of the gospel makes everything else lose color.

Second, this content becomes present reality by serving existentially in the new church formation of my country. *Theologia doloris* serves for *ecclesia doloris* through *existentia doloris*.

Third, this content also ultimately encounters the ethical existence of individuals. (See pages 87-88 of this book.) *Theologia doloris* demands our life as its substance at least in this respect.

K. K., *June 1954*

PREFACE TO THE FIFTH EDITION

As I write a preface to this edition, my deepest concern is about the problem of "existence and dogma." "Existence" means an "outsider" as a "man standing alone before God" and exists outside the universal and the general; this thought of Kierkegaard's is an eternal truth. It is also an unchanging truth that the task of theology is to serve the universal church. Theology becomes dogma when recognized by the universal church.

Should not theology exist ultimately where existence and dogma meet? Athanasius and Luther formulated the dogma recognized by the universal church, though they were rejected by and cast outside the universal-general at the beginning.

The starting point of the theology of the pain of God was to stand "outside" the universal-general, following Jesus who suffered "outside the gate" (Heb. 13:12). (See page 150 of this book.) How does one judge this theology which received such a review as the following one: "Most people received Kitamori's theology as presenting 'answers' rather than 'questions.' In spite of a boom of Kitamori's theology, it appears that this theology did not create a fresh awareness of problems to the Japanese church, nor offer a key to their solution, but rather presented a sort of orthodoxy" (The National Council of Churches, *Church Education*, November 1957, p. 6). One must admit that this theology, while being treated as orthodox doctrine, is still considered as having a characteristic of being "outside." An attempt by some critics to identify this theology with patripassianism is a good example. My theology, however, cannot be identified with patripassianism unless the critics can prove that I made reference to God the Father as the One who suffered on the cross. I cannot understand such a criticism, since there is no proof of this, and moreover since I clearly stated the difference of my position from that of patripassianism on page 115 of this book. Does this not reveal that the theological position of such critics belongs to the *theologia gloriae* (theology of glory) after all?

The theology of the pain of God does not mean that pain exists in God as *substance*. The pain of God is not a "concept of substance"—it is a "concept of relation," a nature of "God's love." Failure to understand this point is the fundamental cause of confusing this theology with patripassianism. The theology of the pain of God will continue to remain "outside" the *theologia gloriae*.

I must make a few remarks in connection with the publication of the Japanese Revised Standard Version of the Bible. This publication made me conscious once again of the "outsidedness" of this theology.

The Japanese Revised Standard Version adopted the translation "My heart yearns over him" (Jer. 31:20). This translation failed to reflect what I have been advocating with concern over the past twenty years. The translation reflects the influence of liberal theology, emphasizing "monisticism of God's love." (See pages 153 ff. of this book.) The meaning of this passage, which Luther and Calvin clearly translated and interpreted as the "pain of God," was distorted to an immediate "love of God." The Japanese Revised Standard Version shows that the word in Jeremiah 31:20 linguistically can be translated in the sense of "pain," as evidenced in the translations of the same Hebrew word in Jeremiah 48:36 as *nageku* ("grieve"), in Psalm 55:17 as *nageki umeku* ("grieve" and "groan"), and in Psalm 77:3 as *nageki kanashimu* ("grieve" and "sorrow"). We can therefore detect a theological bias beyond linguistic grounds in translating Jeremiah 31:20 as *shitau* ("yearn").

The theology of the pain of God will stay "outside" the generally accepted Japanese Revised Standard Version and stand with Luther, Calvin, and the Japanese Literary Version. A wide acceptance of the Japanese Revised Standard Version compels me to use the "pain of God" as a "theological term," recognizing the "outsidedness" of this theology.

I myself do not find the necessity of using the "pain of God" as a theological term any longer, since this term has served its purpose adequately in stressing the mediatory and intercessory love of God over against the immediate love of God. The appearance of the Japanese Revised Standard Version may necessitate my using this term consciously again.

I wish to express my indebtedness to Mr. Hisashi Mine, my student at Tokyo Union Theological Seminary, who compiled the indices at the end of this book.

K. K., *September 1958*

Chapter One

God in Pain

I

We must fathom the "heart of the gospel" by knowing the will of God minutely (Col. 1:9) and by searching the depths of God (1 Cor. 2:10). This petition must become ours, as in the prayer of Kierkegaard:

> Lord! Give us weak eyes
>   for things which are of no account
> and clear eyes
>   for all thy truth.

These "clear eyes" are demanded from those who witness to the gospel. These eyes are sensitive toward theological issues, inasmuch as theology is a witness to the gospel. Without these eyes, a witness is but a visionary; without this sensitivity, a theologian is but a loquacious man.

Since we are dealing with the gospel, it is clear that these eyes —this sensitivity—are given by God alone. They are not our natural eyes and sensitivity, but God's gifts which we do not deserve. We must not hide these gifts under the earth (Matt. 25:18); we must use them (Matt. 25:16), sharpen them, and make them clearer. Certainly it is God who makes them clearer; yet we must seek in prayer that God grant us "clearer eyes."

The heart of the gospel was revealed to me as the "pain of God." This revelation led me to the path which the prophet Jeremiah had trod (Jer. 31:20). Jeremiah was a "man who saw the heart of God most deeply" (Kittel). I am filled with gratitude because I was allowed to experience the depths of God's heart with Jeremiah.

Jeremiah may be called the Paul of the Old Testament; Paul, the Jeremiah of the New. "God on the cross" for Paul is "God in pain" for Jeremiah. God as revealed to Jeremiah served for a prophecy and a witness to God as revealed to Paul. When "God on the cross" is obscured, the theology of "God in pain" will serve in clearing this obscurity away.

Theology is a precise understanding of the gospel. In this sense, Paul who wrote Galations was literally a theologian, for Galatians excels all other writings in its precise understanding of the gospel. We must also call Jeremiah a most precise interpreter of the gospel, for he "saw the heart of God most deeply."

Similarly, the theology of the pain of God attempts to understand the gospel most precisely. My purpose in this book is "to know the will of God minutely" and "to search the depths of God" by following Jeremiah and Paul.

II

God in pain is the God who resolves our human pain by his own. Jesus Christ is the Lord who heals our human wounds by his own (1 Peter 2:24).

This theme contains two important points: (1) Our God is the One who resolves our pain and the Lord who heals. (2) Yet this God is the wounded Lord, having pain in himself. Let us consider these two points.

(1) First of all, we must proclaim that the gospel is indeed "glad tidings." God in the gospel is the One who resolves our pain and the Lord who heals our wounds. This means that he is our "Savior." What is salvation? Salvation is the message that our God enfolds our broken reality. A God who embraces us completely—this is God our Savior. Is there a more astonishing miracle in the world than that God embraces our broken reality? Our reality is utterly and hopelessly broken. Yet the gospel brings us the message of "hope even for the hopeless"—yea, rather "hope *only* for the hopeless." Those who believe in this gospel believe against their own hope (Rom. 4:18). This all-embracing God

resolves our pain and heals our wounds. Accordingly the pain of God which resolves our pain is "love" rooted in his pain. There is reason to believe that the same Hebrew word used in Jeremiah 31:20 and Isaiah 63:15 is translated as "my heart yearns" and "compassion" respectively.

Our Lord's wounds, which heal our wounds, are "Rich wounds, yet visible above,/ In beauty glorified," and the Lord of the cross is at once the Lord of the resurrection. Just as Paul implies "the word of the cross and the resurrection" by his phrase "the word of the cross" (1 Cor. 1:18), so I imply "theology of love rooted in God's pain" by the phrase "theology of the pain of God." Luther calls the death of Christ "death against death" (*mors contra mortem*);[1] I call the pain of God "pain against pain" (*dolor contra dolorem*). Just as "death against death" is the resurrection, so "pain against pain" is God's love which resolves our pain. For this reason, the message of the pain of God is called *glad* tidings.

(2) Why are the glad tidings bound up with the "pain" of God? Why does the Lord who heals our wounds suffer wounds himself? Our reality is such that God ought not to forgive or to enfold it. "I cannot endure . . ." (Isa. 1:13). "I am weary of relenting" (Jer. 15:6). The living and true God must sentence us sinners to death. This is the manifestation of "his wrath." "Thus shall my anger spend itself, and I will vent my fury upon them and satisfy myself; and they shall know that I, the LORD, have spoken in my jealousy, when I spend my fury upon them" (Ezek. 5:13). This wrath of God is absolute and firm. We may say that the recognition of God's wrath is the beginning of wisdom.

The "pain" of God reflects his will to love the object of his wrath. Theodosius Harnack points out that the two elements—the wrath of God and the love of God—produce the "tertiary" (*tertium*).[2] This "tertiary" is the pain of God. Luther sees "God fighting with God" at Golgotha (*da streydet Gott mit Gott*).[3] God who must sentence sinners to death fought with God who wishes to love them. The fact that this fighting God is not two different gods but the same God causes his pain. Here heart is opposed to heart within God.[4] "God opened the way for man's atonement by experiencing unspeakable suffering, going through agonies, and offering himself as sacrifice."[5] The doctrine of atonement is to illumine this process of his agonies.

The Lord wants to heal our wounds, which were caused by God's wrath; this Lord suffers wounds, himself receiving his wrath. ". . . with his stripes we are healed" (Isa. 53:5). The death of Christ is "death of death" (*mors mortis*).[6] The Lord was unable to resolve our death without putting himself to death. God himself was broken, was wounded, and suffered, because he embraced those who should not be embraced. By embracing our reality, God grants us absolute peace. *But the peace has been completely taken away from the Lord who grants us absolute peace.* "My God, my God, why hast thou forsaken me?"

III

A task of the "theology of the pain of God" is to win over the theology which advocates a God who has no pain. As discussed above, the theology of the pain of God deals with two sides of truth, and so our present task also must be directed against the two sides: (1) against the position which rejects the all-embracing God, and (2) against the position which excludes the pain of God from his embracing love.

(1) What was the motif of the theology which was born thirty years ago in the face of world tragedy? This theology saw God in opposition (*Gegenüber*) to man,[7] and its consistent motif was to assert "this fundamental opposition of God and man."[8] To this God in opposition, man is required to become an obedient being (*Gehorsamer*).[9]

What is grace according to this theology? It is "God's proclaiming his works exclusively and independently."[10] What is faith according to this theology? "Faith is awe in the presence of the divine incognito; it is the love of God that is aware of the qualitative distinction between God and man and God and the world; it is the affirmation of the resurrection as the turning-point of the world; and therefore it is the affirmation of the divine 'no' in Christ, of the shattering halt in the presence of God."[11] What is revelation according to this theology? It is ". . . the indicatives that explain the imperative of the First Commandment: Thou shalt have no other gods before me!"[12] The theme of the "revelatory God" lies in its exclusion (*Exklusivität*) of a "general God." "In referring to the exclusiveness of this theme we have perhaps already caught a glimpse of the theme itself: the reality of God that has to do with man, the majesty of that God Who is Father, Son and Holy Ghost and Who cannot yield His honour to another. The indicative in the first commandment is indeed of a certainty no merely formal statement!"[13] According to this theology, the first commandment is the confession of faith which the church should confess today.[14] The first commandment is the theological axiom (*Das erste Gebot als theologische Axiom*).

Even though this theology speaks of the "gospel" as its content, we must admit that the form which determines this content is strictly the law, the first commandment. The prolegomena which reveals the intention of this theology is the "law."

Even though this theology speaks of the "mediator," the theme of the prolegomena as its premise is the opposition of general revelation and special revelation.[15]

The nature of theology is determined by its motif—by its real intention. Opposition, exclusion, qualitative difference, denial, the first commandment—it is evident that the motif consistently emphasized in these expressions is quite different from the motif of the gospel of all-embracing God. We shall not even be surprised to hear the following words from this theology: "God is a total person without tearing and pain" (*ein Ganzes ohne Risse und Schmerzen*).[16] It is obvious that a God who does not embrace is a God without pain.

But we must respond with Paul, "We preach Christ crucified." In the midst of another world tragedy after thirty years, we must envisage God differently from the way he was recognized by the theology of the past generation. The present condition is far more serious than that of thirty years ago, and today's tragedy is taking its final appearance. Therefore the gospel ought to be presented in its most definitive manner.

(2) Albrecht Ritschl once discovered that "an adequate concept of God is expressed in the concept of love," and he rejoiced in the conviction that "the problem of the world could be solved"

by this love of God.[17] We wish, if possible, to rejoice with
Ritschl. The love of God which solves the problem of the world—
is there any more gratifying message than this? Schleiermacher,
Ritschl, Herrmann, and Harnack were all able to sing out loud
this melody of God's love.

— But we, hearing this song, cannot help but say, "Friends, not to
that melody." Here we recall Kierkegaard's beautiful words: "The
birds on the branches, the lilies of the field, the deer in the forest,
the fish of the sea, and numberless happy people are singing, 'God
is love!' But just as a tone of bass sounding beneath these sopra-
nos, the voice of One who was sacrificed echoes from the depths,
De profundis, saying, 'God is love!' " The "love of God" of liberal
theology since Schleiermacher is nothing but the "soprano" of
these happy people. They did not have the ears to hear the bass
which is the pain of God sounding out of the depths.

The "love of God" for them was the *im-mediate* love without
the *mediator*, the pain of God. "To be grasped, filled with the
immediate influence of the universe as with the receptiveness of
children"; "the condition of being embraced by the universe"; that
is, the "marriage" of the finite and the infinite is the "love of God"
that Schleiermacher saw.[18] He very bluntly insists that all doctrines
of the atonement which refer to the blood of Christ are to be
dismissed as "magical."[19] For him the cross of Christ was "dis-
pensable," *entbehrlich*.[20] When Ritschl says, "The reconciliation
of sinners by God . . . can be conceived of *without inconsistency*
with the love of God as a means to building the kingdom of God,"
we cannot be mistaken by what he means.[21] Herrmann jumps to
the conclusion, in spite of his piety, that we can be completely
indifferent to the "mystical atoning power" of Jesus.[22] And
Harnack's famous words are: "The gospel, as Jesus proclaimed it,
has to do with the Father only, and not with the Son."[23] Let me
ask Harnack, by using the words of Jesus from the Synoptic
Gospels which he cherished, ". . . how is it written of the Son of
man, that he should suffer many things and be treated with contempt?" (Mark 9:12). Church history knows no such instances in
which the pain of God was denied on such a large scale as in
liberal theology. Surely since Satan made Peter say, ". . . Lord!

This shall never happen to you" (Matt. 16:22), he has never been
at work so hard as in liberalism.

The above two views, in spite of their diametric opposition to
each other, are both alike in being unable to meet reality for us.
By this, I mean that they are unable to save us. To make this point
clear, we must "persuade."

But since this persuasion is accomplished through the theology
of the pain of God, it must also mean "acceptance" as well. We
noted that God in pain is completely the One who enfolds. If God
only persuades others from the opposing position, it implies the
loss of his essence. The theology of the pain of God must, ultimately, enfold the opposition and win it to his side. This is "acceptance." This means not just to embrace the opposition, but to
make it aware of its abstract nature, change its course, and transform it to the concrete truth. "Persuasion" is "acceptance."

IV

We cannot believe the pain of God unless it is his revelation.
Man's thought can never produce such a truth. Accordingly, the
pain of God can exist as a truth only in the framework of theology; it cannot spring from man's philosophical or religious thinking. Nevertheless, the deepest thoughts the world has ever pro-
duced, unknowingly, have searched for the pain of God. These
thoughts attempt to tune their melody to that of the pain of God.
When each thought in its quest comes close to the note of the pain
of God, it can be called a profound thought. Unfortunately, we
must respond to such a thought, "Friends, not to that melody,"
as long as it remains a human concept. However, we must admit
that such a thought is most precious and valuable in our world.
Let us examine two or three such representative thoughts which
are most profound in the above sense.

First, the later philosophy of Schelling should be mentioned:
the idea of *nature in God* (*Natur in Gott*) as developed in *The
Essence of Human Freedom*. Schelling saw "what is not God in
God himself."[24] This is "nature in God," "indispensable yet
different being." This "nature in God" is his basis, which is distinct from his essence: his essence is his will to love, and his basis

is his will to anger. "The absolute being divides himself into two beings according to his works." "God as spirit" is "the absolute unity of these two principles." God's spirit is actually nothing but "God as love" in the highest sense of the word.[25] This thought of Schelling's comes within a hairbreadth of truth, so long as it points to the gospel, bringing about the pain of God as a synthesis of his wrath and love. Schelling even says "that all of history is virtually an enigma without a concept of an *agonizing God*."[26] And again, "this is because any essence becomes clearer only in the face of its opposite. Unless there is division in principle, unity cannot witness to its omnipotence. Unless there is discord, love actually cannot exist."[27] But Schelling was only a philosophical searcher whose characteristics are that he, though coming close to the truth, departs from it again. Since Schelling never discovered the pain of God, he did not remain as one who witnesses to it, but rather went on to speculate about the "explanation of evil." It is obvious that in his philosophy Schelling was most confused in his explanation of evil. Here one no longer feels the compelling pull of truth, but the fetid atmosphere of confusion. This kind of thinking is not completely absent even in the "nature of God." We must say, "Friends, not to that melody"!

Second, the religious thought closest to the gospel—the pain of God which heals our wounds—is found in the Crown Prince Shotoku's *An Interpretation of the Yuimakyo*, where we find religious thought which closely resembles our gospel of the pain of God who heals our pain.[28] There we find the earth-shaking sentence: "Man's real sickness springs from foolish love; Buddha's responding sickness arises from great mercy." Buddha's sickness-in-response "comes from his suffering mercy. His suffering mercy is man's vice—man's sickness. The sickness of the great mercy saves people by absorbing their sickness. Sickness is saved by sickness."[29] The thought closest to the gospel which claims "the wound is healed by the wound" is found in the expression "Sickness is saved by sickness." We are exceedingly grateful to the revered religious ancestors of our native country who entertained these ideas. I believe that Japanese thought became deeper after the adoption of the above idea.

However, it must not be overlooked that in this religious thought the echo of an alien note is heard. The sickness of the great mercy is always responding sickness, and never real sickness. Therefore it is said that the Buddha is "constantly in repose and never in repose." "The sickness of the great mercy is called sickness, but actually is not sickness."[30] Why did this thought arise? Because, after all, this religious thought is Buddhist. There can be no inflexible wrath of the absolute in Buddhism, as long as it does not have the God of the first commandment. An absolute being without wrath can have no *real* pain. The word "sorrow," as used in composing the term "great mercy" in Oriental language, simply means "sympathy," and cannot be regarded in the same way as our "pain." The pain of God is his love—this love is based on the premise of his wrath, which is absolute, inflexible reality. Thus the pain of God is *real* pain, the Lord's wounds are *real* wounds. Buddhism cannot comprehend this real pain, even in the stages of thought of the Jodo and Jodo Shinshu sects about the mercy of Amida Buddha. Here again, "Friends, not to that melody"!

Third, Hegel's philosophy of history must be examined. The thought (rather, the faith!) which Hegel developed in *Reason in History* was that reason rules the world and thus world history is rational. In religious terms, this means the providence of God rules the world; in our terminology, God completely embraces our reality. Of course Hegel derived this thought from his Christian background, but he developed it strictly as his own philosophy. In this respect it is not theology, but a philosophical search. In Japanese philosophical circles this idea of Hegel's is quite unpopular because of its abstractness as "teleological determinism." But the greatness of Hegel's thought is not injured by this criticism, nor are Japanese philosophies more concrete. I believe that Hegel's thought should be *vitalized* today. We cannot ignore Hegel's thought if philosophy is to exercise any sort of power. Hegel indicated by this thought the primary issue in the theology of the pain of God: God completely embraces our reality.

Unfortunately, however, Hegel lost sight of the *second* point in developing the primary one. In the gospel message, God *suffers* pain because he embraces. But in Hegel, God *does not suffer* pain although he embraces. Even if Hegel's God allows individuals to wound one another, he remains a universal being, undisturbed and invulnerable. This God protects himself from being disturbed by "cunning of reason" (*List der Vernunft*). By cunning of reason, Hegel's God never suffers wounds. Thus the abstractness of Hegel's philosophy lies not in his portrayal of God as embracing the world, but in his portrayal of God as a being without pain. Because of this abstractness, Hegel's rationalism cannot bring salvation to our reality. Here again, "Friends, not to that melody"!

What attitude should the theology of the pain of God take toward the thoughts outlined above, which suggest in a groping way this theology? Since these thoughts are but "thoughts," should theology condemn them all as being vain? Doubtless such an attitude could be adopted were theology not the theology of the pain of God. But as long as it is the theology of the *pain* of God it cannot take this attitude. This theology regards such ideas with infinite love, extending itself to approach them, and praying that they will touch it. The theology of the pain of God, only when it adopts this attitude, becomes truth which lives its name.

V

The theology of the pain of God claims to be a true science. Let us now discuss two points concerning the character of this theology as science.

1. Although Hegel recognized that religion and philosophy have the same object, he believed religion apprehended this object by the method of representation (*Vorstellung*), whereas philosophy used the concept (*Begriff*), which Hegel regarded as superior. According to this logic, the expression "pain of God" has not yet emerged from the stage of representation, and we must find the corresponding *concept* to such a representation in an effort to define this theology strictly as science. One might insist that such an expression as "pain of God" should be abandoned when a corresponding concept is found.

But would such an insistence be correct? The precision of science should not move in that direction when it is concerned with the gospel. If a concept equivalent to the pain of God be sought in Hegelian manner, such concepts as the "negation of negation," "absolute negation," or "absolute affirmation" might be found. But if the "pain of God" is to be replaced by some such concept, the gospel would no longer be defined precisely, but on the contrary imprecisely. The closer a science adheres to its situation, the more precise it becomes. When some philosophical concept attempts to define the gospel, the gospel loses its decisiveness. Thus the scientific grasp of the situation becomes imprecise. The decisiveness of the gospel is expressed only by such a term as the "pain of God." Even if the "pain of God" and the "negation of negation" are alike in form of expression, the latter does not possess the same quality. In the gospel—and, for that matter, in every absolute— quality is decisive. The expression indicating quality in itself brings precision to science. This is the distinctive nature of theology as science. Theology never stands on the same level as what Hegel calls "religion." In discussing an ultimate and absolute, theology insists on a precision which criticizes philosophical "concepts" as imprecise. The "pain of God" certainly is not what Hegel calls "representation."

We cannot help feeling that such expressions as the "pain of God" already transcend the dimensions of "representation" which are subordinate to "concepts." We see this in the following philosophical sentences:

"While mediation is limited by that which is mediated, and to that extent is negated, yet it is affirmed by mediating the negation and thus it retains its autonomy. At the same time, that which is mediated recognizes the freedom of the mediator. In the freedom of self-will, the mediator accepts negation from the resistance of the mediated and yet makes his own 'wound' the negative turning point of love, which is positive mediation.

"The mediator, wounded and hurt by resistance which is the fundamental evil of the individual, must nevertheless accept the individual and be summoned so that he will be converted voluntarily. Thus this mediation is called mercy or love. The absolute, which transcends man's sin without pain and suffering, may be called love, God, mercy, or Buddha, yet it does not satisfy our religious needs; its universality ends as unmediated comprehensiveness and cannot be concrete in the sense of absolute mediation.

"But, Hegel understands individual freedom and particularly his self-will as a means of attaining the absolute universal idea, as shown in the above-mentioned concept of the 'cunning of reason.' This is clearly a denial of Kant's self-purposiveness of personality. Kant, therefore, does not give adequately positive meaning to man's fundamental evil and tends to stop at the suggestion of the limitation and abstractness of the particular as opposed to the universal. In raising and bringing the particular to salvation, the absolute does not require the mediation of the ascending and descending movement: by means of the negation and limitation to itself, pained and grieving through the individual's arbitrary turning away from it, the mediator descends to the status of the individual, accepting it and raising it to an absolute good."[31]

The stage reached in the above quotation surpasses that of the following: "The light which embraces the darkness from its depths is true reason. The love which loves an enemy is true love. Such love alone supports absolute dialectical reason emotionally."[32]

2. Restraint in words must be regarded as a human virtue. In a science which aims at precision, this virtue must be displayed if possible. Can we not display this virtue in theology? Specifically, cannot a more restrained word than the crude term "pain" of God be used?

No, we cannot. In all other human affairs restraint in words is possible, even desirable. Since all human affairs are *immanent* for both the speaker and the listener, it is possible to *draw out* the matter in question by the use of restrained words. It may be more effective if the words are restrained.

But the circumstances are completely different when the gospel concerning God is in question. Since the affairs of God are transcendental, for both the speaker and the listener, it is infinitely difficult to draw out the meaning, even by the most skillful use of words. Witnessing for the gospel demands our tackling of this difficulty. How is it possible for this kind of testimony to afford the aesthetic attitude of using restraint in expression? Theology, as precise understanding of the gospel, must be aware that it cannot display such an aesthetic virtue. In this sense theology may be called "crude"; it must endure this humiliation. But how can one who is conscious of "crudeness," and knows indignity, be crude? The "crudeness" of theology is far superior to any human "refinement."

Using words with restraint and controlling one's feelings are virtues of the Japanese. But the Japanese virtue is not limited to these aspects. We must give careful attention to Norinaga Motoori's words in connection with the misfortunes of Prince Yamato Takeru: "The prince maintained a brave mind and accomplished his great work, faithfully fulfilling the command of his father the Emperor. But at the same time he revealed the resentment he felt toward his father and wept over grievous things: This should be called the true heart of a man. Had a Chinese been in a similar position, he would have tried to conceal his resentment or grief, however deeply he might feel it in his heart, and would ordinarily try to carry it off by speaking heroic words. From this you may conclude what a great difference there is in every respect between mere foreigners, who easily keep up appearances, and the ancient people of our empire, who were true to their hearts."[33] The Japanese way is to "grieve and weep for those things which should be grieved over" and not to "wrap up and hide their color."

Chapter Two

The Pain of God
and the Historical Jesus

I

Paul did not know Christ "after the flesh" (*kata sarka*) (II Cor.
5:16, K.J.V.), yet he definitely knew him "in the flesh" (*en te sarki*)
(Rom. 8:3). The relationship between the pain of God and the
historical Jesus can be clarified if these two aspects of Jesus Christ
are fully retained. When we see only the historical Jesus, not the
pain of God, we have known Christ "after the flesh" only. When
we see only the pain of God, not the historical Jesus, we have lost
sight of Christ "in the flesh." I have explained this problem fully
on a previous occasion:

> The gospel is fact, the fact of that "which we have heard,
> which we have seen with our eyes, which we have looked upon
> and touched with our hands." The gospel is fact because it
> happened outside of our thoughts, emotions, and experiences—
> that is, outside of ourselves. The gospel is an event that happened
> once for all, and it cannot be repeated. It is a fact represented by
> the name "Jesus Christ." Even if somewhere in the world there
> were a religious thought with almost the same content as the
> gospel of Jesus Christ, it would not be the gospel if it did not bear
> his name. The name of Jesus Christ is a fact that stands outside
> our ideas, our religious feelings, and our philosophies. None of
> these can adjust this objective fact to his convenience. The gospel
> stands outside us as a fact—this is certainly the truth.
> Here we must turn our eyes to a yet deeper truth. Certainly
> the gospel is a fact, yet it is not a mere fact but *fact as gospel*.

The gospel is the fact that God *loves* us, the fact of God's love. And the love of God exists only when we ourselves are included in it. That is, the gospel is not only a fact that stands outside us, but a fact which *enfolds* us. We cannot think of the gospel represented by the name of Jesus Christ apart from God's love for us. The love of God alone establishes the fact of the *gospel.* This is why we have indicated that Jesus Christ is "love rooted in the pain of God."

One thing is clear: It is abstract and false to think of the fact of Jesus Christ apart from the love of God. The gospel is not a mere *objective* fact standing outside us; it is at the same time a *subjective* fact always including us. The fact of Jesus Christ is always the fact of *faith*, because faith means we are enfolded in the love of God. The fact of Jesus Christ, seen merely objectively, not as faith sees it, is no longer the fact of the *gospel.* Seen objectively, apart from the love of God, the birth of Jesus is simply the birth of the founder of a religion; the cross of Jesus is the miserable death of an idealist; and the resurrection of Jesus is an illusion to which fanaticism gave birth. The fact of Jesus Christ becomes the fact of the gospel only when seen as the fact of the *love of God* enfolding us. Only when the birth and death of Jesus Christ are seen as the "pain of God" and his resurrection as the "love [rooted in the pain] of God" do these facts become the fact of the gospel. Only here can *truth* be found. Only he who *believes* sees the truth.[1]

One may say that the above discussion is moving "from the historical Jesus to the *pain of God*," that is, in one direction only. For this reason, these ideas need supplementation. One must also move in the opposite direction: "from the pain of God to the *historical Jesus.*"

At this point it is necessary to rethink carefully the well-known claim of Wrede. According to Wrede, Paul's belief in Christ as the heavenly being preceded his belief in the historical Jesus. "Thus the man Jesus simply bore all those mighty predicates he had already possessed."[2] "Paul, a Pharisee, transferred to the historical Jesus his preconceived concepts of a divine being."[3] "Jesus did not know what Paul conceived to be absolute and ultimate."[4] "The name 'disciple of Jesus' has little applicability to Paul if it is used to denote a historical relationship."[5] In short, according to Wrede, "the picture of Christ did not originate in an impression of the personality of Jesus."[6]

This claim is one-sided and reveals the hastiness and narrowness frequently characterizing scholars with originality. Nevertheless, this claim does not lose its significance and value. It makes us move consciously, in the Pauline way of thinking, from the pain of God toward the *historical Jesus*. In light of this, we must rethink the significance *originally* attached to historical Jesus.

Recognition of the significance originally attached to the historical Jesus is a new task for today's theology. But for us this path is inevitably *"from* the pain of God *toward* the historical Jesus," and not simply *"to* the historical Jesus." In the conclusion of *Paulus*, Wrede spoke of "comprehending and evaluating Paul from a purely historical point of view," [7] but in this respect we are not in agreement with Wrede. This disagreement becomes quite apparent in the above passage from my earlier book.

"From the pain of God toward the historical Jesus" means a recognition of the historical Jesus as a necessary constituent factor in the pain of God. This by no means indicates that the "meaning" of the historical Jesus is the pain of God and that the "realization" of the pain of God is the historical Jesus. It means that the necessity of the historical Jesus is implied in the pain of God.

> An example of this train of thought is Anselm's ontological evidence for the existence of God. Here the existence of God as a fact is not to be sought apart from the concept of God, but in the very concept itself. In the concept of "God" his existence as a fact is included as a necessary constituent factor of the concept. Similarly, in the concept of the pain of God, the existence of the historical Jesus, which seems contrary to the concept, is included as a necessary constituent factor of the concept. Just as the concept of "God" cannot be established without his existence as fact, so the concept of the pain of God cannot be established without the historicity of Jesus. Concretely, what does this imply?

The pain of God means that the love of God had conquered the wrath of God in the midst of the *historical* world deserving his wrath. Thus the pain of God must *necessarily* enter the historical plane as a person. This is the truth recorded in Romans 8:3: ". . . sending his own Son in the likeness of sinful flesh and for sin, he condemned sin in the flesh." The pain of God could not have existed had not the Redeemer, the personification of God's pain, been a historical figure. In Luther's words, the pain of God deals with "real sin" (*verum peccatum*), and not "imaginary sin" (*fictum peccatum*).[8] Only the historical world is the world of real sin; any ideational world is the world of imaginary sin. Jesus, the personification of the pain of God, assumed the "flesh" of this historical world. Jesus "in the flesh" was "real man," a *historical* person. God himself had to enter the world of real sin in order to bear the responsibility of real sin.

Every form of docetism results in a denial of the pain of God. The assertion that Jesus was not a real historical person implies his existence in some ideational world. Real sin does not exist in an ideational world. When sin becomes an idea, we cease to hate (Titus 3:3) such sin. As Augustine says, "Sin is something which should never be forgiven," but imaginary sin is already something that "can be forgiven." Forgiveness for a forgivable sin is a denial of the pain of God. The pain of God is his love conquering the inflexible wrath of God, but this wrath of God does not arise against an ideational world.

Only the pain of God can deny fundamentally every sort of docetism. It is now clear that the concept of the pain of God upholds the significance originally attached to the historical Jesus.

The path which we have traversed "from the pain of God toward the historical Jesus" assumes the path "from the historical Jesus toward the pain of God" as well. The pain of God is in the infinitely deep background of the historical Jesus. Any theories lack depth without this background. Any Christology of the Mediator lacks depth without insight of this background.

II

The problem of the historical Jesus concerns not only his person, but also his teaching. This is seen most acutely in Harnack's emphasis on the "twofold gospel" in *What Is Christianity?* He distinguishes the "gospel *of* Jesus" from the "gospel *about* Jesus." The former refers to the religion of Jesus himself with the central themes "God the Father," the "coming of the Kingdom of God," and the "higher righteousness." The latter is the Pauline religion with the central theme of the redemption of man through the death and resurrection of Jesus Christ. Wrede had already recognized such a sharp contrast between these two: "Those who attempt to portray the religion that lives in the discourses and parables of Jesus never think of discussing the religion of atonement."[9] According to Wrede, Paul had moved further away from Jesus than Jesus had moved from the Jewish religion.[10] "Jesus or Paul: this alternative characterizes, at least in part, the religious and theological battle of the present day."[11]

"Jesus or Paul": the significance of this proposition lies in its attempt to uphold the original nature of the teaching of the historical Jesus. As is well known, the churches and theological circles were severely shocked when this problem was presented half a century ago. The shock waves gradually subsided, and the whole problem seems to be forgotten today. Is it not true that this problem yet remains unsolved? At least I have never heard a clear and precise answer to the problem. It must be our common task, then, to make efforts, no matter how small, toward a solution. I have already expressed some of my own ideas concerning this problem in my previous writing,[12] and I shall just present some of the main points here.

Contrasted with Pauline teaching, the main characteristic of the teaching of Jesus revealed in the Synoptic Gospels is the superiority with which the *intent love of God* is taught. Thus an expression such as "Jesus' serene view of God" is used. In contrast, Paulinism speaks of the love of God, but only in the context of the painful process of the atonement of Jesus Christ. Here the love of God is definitely based on the *pain of God*. Accordingly the contrast between Jesus and Paul is essentially the contrast between the love of God and the pain of God. But does this contrast mean an *opposition* between the two? Here lies the crux of the problem. Does Jesus' teaching on the love of God originate in the pain of God which Paul saw in Jesus? The pain of God which Paul saw implies the *person* of Jesus Christ. Therefore, to say that the teaching of Jesus is based on Paul's teaching shows that Jesus' teaching is based on his own person. This is "love rooted in the pain of God." Nothing could be more natural than this—the teaching is based on the person who taught it.

We must think more deeply on this. As long as we are sinners—
and this fact is recognized by *Jesus* and Paul—we do not receive
God's love. Rather, the love of God becomes the wrath of God in
his response to sin (and this is recognized by *Jesus* and Paul). But
God loved us, the objects of this wrath. The pain of God is his
love which conquered this wrath. Paul actually saw the pain of
God in the person of Jesus Christ. But we must note that Jesus
also spoke clearly of this pain and related it to his own person: in
Matthew 9:13 (Mark 2:17; Luke 5:31); Matthew 16:21-23
(Mark 8:31-33; Luke 9:22); Matthew 17:9-13 (Mark 9:9-13);
Matthew 17:22; Matthew 20:28 (Mark 10:45); Matthew 26:6-
13 (Mark 14:3-9); Matthew 26:24 (Mark 14:21; Luke 22:22);
Matthew 26:26-29 (Mark 14:22-25; Luke 22:15-20); Matthew 26:
42, 54; Mark 9:12; Luke 7:41-50; 9:44; 13:6-9; 15:1-32; 18:9-14;
19:1-10; 23:34, 39-43. We can say that these passages contain the
same viewpoint as Paul's. (Remaining aspects of the problem will
be discussed later.)

Sinners are won to complete obedience to God by his love—
that is, his pain—which reaches those turning their backs on
God's love. If one is obedient, he cannot be separated from the
love of God, and one can no longer be separated from the pain of
God which captures sinners. What is happening here is the victory
of God over sinners. The victory is that of a love which completely penetrates and goes through the pain, a love rooted in the
pain of God. What is called "Jesus' serene view of God" must
mean this intent love of God. In Jesus this love is revealed in two
forms: the first in connection with ethics, the second, with happiness.

The ethical commandments of Jesus can only exist in the intent
love of God. It is impossible for them to exist within the immediate love of God which has not been penetrated by the pain of
God. The love of God, reflected in the lilies of the field and the
birds of the air, is the source of true happiness when it is applied
to man, but this is also possible within God's intent love. In the
wrath of God which has not penetrated his pain, we may call this
appearance of God an illusion. It is only possible to show this
form of God in Jesus. "Almost all Christ's moral precepts might

be paralleled or illustrated by something in Hebrew or Jewish literature. This praise of the beauty of flowers cannot, apparently, be so paralleled. . . . Of all Christ's sayings it is the most original."[13] Today we must make this original characteristic of Jesus' teaching fully alive. So much, then, toward a solution of the problem of "Jesus and Paul."

We are in debt to Wrede, Harnack, and other liberal theologians for their calling our attention to this fact; here lies their theological significance. However, I believe they were mistaken on two points:

1. Liberalism regarded God's love revealed in Jesus as *immediate* (im-mediate) love; this exists without a mediator. Paul said this view makes "Christ [to have] died to no purpose" (Gal. 2:21). This make God's love completely *natural*, as for instance in Matthew 5:45; 6:25 ff., where God's love is taught as being revealed in "nature."[14] Here God's love can exist *without* Jesus Christ; Jesus had simply grasped this love, and did no more than convey it to men. What can exist without Christ is, strictly speaking, not Christianity at all. Therefore Harnack's *The Essence of Christianity* actually shows the essence of what is *not* Christianity. The Catholic theologian Denifle's criticism of *The Essence of Christianity*—"his Christianity is *no* Christianity"—is more than sarcasm: it contains the truth.[15]

As noted in Section III of the previous chapter, the essence of liberalism is a negation of the pain of God. The problems raised concerning the historical Jesus are actually variations of this fundamental view. We must reply to this view with the "No!" of conviction. To recognize and vitalize the original characteristics of the intent love of God in Jesus' teaching is to accept and redeem the intention of liberalism. As a word, God's love, rooted in pain, is exactly the same "love" as immediate love. We may interpret this as the recovery of the immediate love through pain. The words of Jesus: "Think not that I have come to abolish the law and the prophets; I have come not to abolish them but to fulfil them" (Matt. 5:17), and Paul's words: "Do we then overthrow the law by this faith? By no means! On the contrary, we uphold the law" (Rom. 3:31) are helpful at this point. The theology of the pain of God must above all be a *theology of answer*, not simply of quest.

> The birds of the air and the lilies of the field in Matthew 6:25 ff. certainly symbolize love rooted in the pain of God, yet we cannot deny that they reflect the immediate love of God, that is, the scenery of nature. Here grace itself speaks through nature. Nature as the immediate love of God is restored and vitalized through the pain of God. In love rooted in the pain of God, the beauty of nature is perceived in its original characteristic.

2. In the thought of both Jesus and Paul, the pain of God and the love of God indissolubly unite to form a unity in the "love rooted in pain"; the pain of God and the love of God are in no sense divided in opposition. The extreme abstractness of liberalism failed to perceive this. We have noted that Jesus taught the pain of God as well as the love of God. We should note here that Paul also deeply comprehends and teaches the love of God as well as the pain of God. It will suffice to mention as specific passages three chapters: Romans 8, 1 Corinthians 13, and 15. In addition, there are numerous examples of Paul's words along these two lines: the very warm ethical solicitude, the absolute peace, joy, and thanksgiving which nothing can take away. Though the form of expression may seem different from that of Jesus, the truth is the same. Paul's matchless greatness is revealed in his embodiment in a seamless fabric of the whole of love rooted in the pain of God. Thus even a man like Luther could not match Paul's concreteness. The failure of the liberals to grasp the importance of this point makes us doubt the adequacy of their theological sense.

III

In the above discussion we have reached a solution to the problem of the relationship of the historical Jesus to his teaching, but two dubious points still require clarification. Jesus spoke about both the pain of God and the love of God, but why did he not speak as explicitly as did Paul? And why does the proclamation of the love of God suggest this love is superior to the pain of God?

Unless these two questions are answered, the problems raised by liberalism have not been answered adequately.

The first point can be answered as follows. The reason why Jesus did not set forth the *significance* of the cross as explicitly as Paul did was that this truth could not be revealed until after the descent of the *Holy Spirit* following the death, resurrection, and ascension of Jesus (John 14:26; 15:26; 16:7, 13). Therefore Jesus entrusted to the apostles the full manifestation of this truth. "The apostolic inspiration is the posthumous exposition by Christ of His own work . . ."[16] It was the disciples who *proclaimed* the truth of the cross. Jesus himself could not adequately speak about this—he only *acted* it. "His thoughts about his death were unutterable, except in an act . . ."[17]

The second problem requires further consideration. Why does Jesus' teaching seem to place the love of God above the pain of God when Jesus is the very pain of God?

The pain of God is the forgiveness of sins. I believe that the solution to this second problem lies in the essence of this forgiveness. To forgive is to forget. One has not forgiven if he says, "I have forgiven, but not forgotten." Has one forgiven his neighbor's sin if he remembers it bitterly and continues to speak of it? And can the forgiven one really enjoy the peace of forgiveness? When one truly forgives, he must forget the fact of his forgiveness. This certainly does not imply that forgiveness is easy tolerance. One must bear responsibility for the sinner and suffer pain. However, the pain, if real, penetrates the one who forgives, and issues forth in intent love. One is not really forgiving others as long as he complains about his own pain in forgiveness. Forgiveness exhibits its true nature, and pain proves to be real, only when intent love enfolds others, forgetting its pain.

This explains why the love of God is placed above the pain of God in the historical Jesus. It is clear that Jesus as the Savior and the personification of God's plan did not explain at length salvation and God's pain; he rather concentrated on offering the solution to man's tragedy and rejoiced in the fulfillment of God's love. This is seen clearly by the fact that one of the Gospels reveals Jesus beginning his public ministry by healing sickness (Mark 1:32-

34). Here Jesus' graciousness of grace is deeply felt. The liberal view which makes Jesus a poet of "God's immediate love" without the above insight is superficial from the human standpoint, and is not worthy of consideration as a theological problem. The love of God is the love *rooted in his pain,* as clearly seen in Mark 2:1-12.

We are told that whereas Paul's gospel was the "gospel of the cross," Jesus' gospel was the "gospel of the Kingdom of God." This is certainly true. But what, essentially, is the Kingdom of God? The Kingdom of God is the *reign of God's love.* If so, the difference between these two gospels is nothing more than the variation of correlates, and a similar solution can be found for them. The problem here is: Can the Kingdom of God be thought of as general truth without Jesus Christ? Liberalism tends to explain it simply as general truth. "When He declared the Kingdom of God is at hand he was not speaking out of apocalyptic calculation, but from His assurance that through Him God was about to exercise the sovereign sway of His good purpose. . . . He regarded His own death as a vital stage in the fulfilment of God's purpose. . . . This confidence in the power and goodness of God is bound up with the person of Jesus Christ. The eschatological hope anticipates a future in which the bliss and relief are mediated through the divine Christ; God is reigning over a people for whom Jesus has given His life as ransom, for whom He has shed His blood, to bring them into the new relationship of sons to the heavenly Father."[18]

IV

The Gospel of John is always a problem when one considers the historical Jesus, for the portrayal of the historicity of Jesus in this Gospel is questionable. Our above discussion certainly provides help for a solution. The fact of Jesus is not a mere fact but *fact as gospel.* The gospel is a historical fact, but it is more than a historical fact. It has an infinitely deep background behind the historical fact. Whereas the Synoptic Gospels draw attention mainly to the foreground of the historical fact, the Gospel of John concentrates attention chiefly on the background of the gospel fact. To see only the foreground as factual, and not the background, is not to consider the fact-as-gospel, and therefore not to think of Jesus Christ.

I have no intention here of discussing the contents of John as a whole. I only wish to consider the way the pain of God as the background of the gospel is presented in the Fourth Gospel. As I see it, this Gospel has a distinctive and consistent theme of the pain of God. This treatment is peculiar to John; there is nothing parallel to it even in Paul. This theme is unfolded in the following passages:

(1) "But Jesus answered them, 'My Father is working still, and I am working.' This was why the Jews sought all the more to kill him, because he not only broke the sabbath but also called God his Father, making himself equal with God" (5:17-18).

(2) " 'I know him, for I come from him, and he sent me.' So they sought to arrest him . . ." (7:29-30).

(3) "Jesus said to them, 'Truly, truly, I say to you, before Abraham was, I am.' So they took up stones to throw at him; but Jesus hid himself, and went out of the temple" (8:58-59).

(4) " 'I and the Father are one.' The Jews took up stones again to stone him. Jesus answered them, 'I have shown you many good works from the Father; for which of these do you stone me?' The Jews answered him, 'We stone you for no good work but for blasphemy; because you, being a man, make yourself God' " (10: 30-33).

(5) "The Jews answered him, 'We have a law, and by that law he ought to die, because he has made himself the Son of God' " (19:7).

The above quotations are linked together by one common factor which could be called the course of destiny. This course proceeds in the following order:

1. Jesus is the *Son of God* and is God himself.

2. Jesus speaks about this.

3. The assertion of Jesus becomes, consequently, the *cause of death* for him.

For Jesus this course was his destiny, a tragic destiny. How tragic it was for the Son of God—God himself—that his own utterance became the cause of his death. This fact is exactly the pain of God. The whole life of Jesus was a way of pain (*via dolorosa*). The act of God's entering into the world itself already implied his death. Not his death, but his birth meant the pain of God for Christ. "He consented not only to die but to be born."[19]

There is a tendency in theological circles today to emphasize John 1:14 alone, but without John 3:16 the former is incomprehensible. And, according to Luther, John 3:16 is the "tragic word" (*tragica verba*).[20] Without apprehension of this tragic love of God, all talk of "the Word made flesh" is empty formalism. It is regrettable to see the tendency toward this formalism in theological circles today. However correct the form, it is false if the content is extracted. The form should not control the content; the *content* must control the form. This is why we must proclaim the "theology of the pain of God" against the so-called "theology of the Word of God."

Chapter Three

Pain as the Essence of God

The task of witnessing to the gospel is to vitalize the *astonishing fact* of the gospel. The message "the Son of God has died" is indeed most astonishing. "It is impossible for us to understand the logic of Paul completely unless the death of Christ means the death of God himself."[1] God has died! If this does not startle us, what will? The church must keep this astonishment alive. The church ceases to exist when she loses this astonishment. Theology, the precise understanding of the gospel, must be seized by this astonishment more than anyone else. It is said that philosophy begins with wonder; so theology begins with wonder. The wonder of philosophy pales before the wonder of theology. The person astonished by the tidings "God has died" can no longer be astonished at anything else.

But the church and theology have long ceased to wonder at this message. The fact that man is no longer astonished by the news "the Son of God died on the cross" is most saddening. This is indeed astonishing. "Be appalled, O heavens, at this, be shocked ..." (Jer. 2:12). The most urgent business before the church and theology today is the recovery of wonder, the pronouncement of the gospel afresh in order to make this wonder vivid again.

I discovered this wonder through Jeremiah 31:20. It was the discovery of "God in pain." Another wonder struck me when I read Hebrews 2:10: "For it was *fitting* that he, for whom and by whom all things exist, in bringing many sons to glory, should make the pioneer of their salvation perfect through suffering." The little word *eprepen* thundered in my ears as though it would shake the entire universe. We enter into the *mysteries* of God by the light of this little word. This word gives us a glimpse of a world which is no longer a world of human beings or of history, but a *world within God*—the world of the "essence of God" in the classical term. We gaze at this with awe.

In a church that has lost this wonder, unastonishing theological doctrines teach that God, against his nature, took an emergency measure and made Christ suffer for the redemption of sin. But according to Hebrews 2:10, it was *fitting* for God to perfect Christ through suffering. Moreover the God spoken of here is "he for whom and by whom all things exist," God in his essential nature. We conclude from this that God's pain was fitting for him. "To be fitting" means to be necessary to his essence. The pain of God is part of his essence! This is really the wonder. God's essence corresponds to his eternity. The Bible reveals that the pain of God belongs to his *eternal being*. "I am the first and the last, and the living one; *I died*, and behold I am alive for evermore" (Rev. 1:17-18). God, who will appear in the ultimate form of his glory, calls himself "the first and the last, *who died* and came to life" (Rev. 2:8). Revelation 13:8 can be translated, "the Lamb slain from the creation of the world." (Further, see where "the Lamb that was slain" appears: Revelation 5:6, 12, 13.)

The cross is in no sense an external act of God, but an act within himself. "The cross was the reflection (or say rather the historic pole) of an act within Godhead."[2] Luther insists that the premise is that "the absolute necessity for the sacrifice of the Son is grounded in God himself" (*eine absolute, innergöttlich begründete Notwendigkeit der Dahingabe des Sohnes*). The question in regard to the salvation of the world, according to him, is not the relation between God and the world, or God and Satan, but the relation between *God* and *God to the world*.[3] "It is not this or that abstract attribute of God, but *God* standing over against *God*: God in his will of wrath and God in his will of love."[4] Therefore, according to Luther, "the gospel was proclaimed even before the foundation of the world, as far as God is concerned."[5]

Eternity accompanies necessity. "The Son of God himself had to become man and to take upon himself sin, the wrath of God, and death."[6]

II

I have just used the term "essence." In the classical theology of the church, the word "essence" played a decisive role. In Trinitarian theology God was expressed as the "essence" (*ousia, substantia*). The truth represented by this term is the mystery of all mysteries. Of all the theological terms ever used, few were so lofty as this. At the same time, however, few were so problematic as this. Indeed, the loftier the term, the more problematic it becomes.

Frankly, no concept is so *remote* from the biblical concept of God as "essence." Those who know God as revealed to Jeremiah and Paul notice immediately that God defined as "essence" is missing one vital point: his *real* essence, his true heart. The pain of God which Jeremiah saw, the love in the cross which Paul saw—this is the essence of God, this is the heart of God. Consequently, the "essence" of God presented in classical Trinitarian doctrine may be called an *essence without essence*.

Recovering this lost essence, I firmly believe, is the ultimate and grave task for today's theology, especially in Japan. The concept of God as "essence without essence" was influenced by Greek thought. Here we see the classical role of the Greek way of thinking in Christian theology. As far as the *concept of God* is concerned, there has never appeared any thought pattern comparable to that of the Greek. It is in this area that the Japanese church must do its deepest thinking. Theology is ultimately concerned with the concept of God. A theology failing to contribute anything decisive to the view of God should not make any final pronouncements.

III

In classical theology, the action of God within his "essence" was regarded as the action of the *immanent Trinity*. This was called *opera trinitatis ad intra*. God the Father *begets* God the

Son, then from God the Father and God the Son proceeds God the Holy Spirit. *Generatio* and *processio* were the basics for this action. The question immediately concerning us is "begetting."

Just as God the "essence" was the "essence without essence," so the act of God in "begetting" is an act which has not yet accomplished his ultimate action. The God revealed to Jeremiah and Paul—the God of the gospel—is not *merely* God the Father who begets his Son. The God of the gospel causes his Son to die and suffers pain in that act. The Father causes his beloved Son, his only begotten Son, to die—this is the ultimate act of God. Classical Trinitarianism saw God only as the Father begetting his Son. Just as God as "essence" lacks something decisive, so God the Father who simply begets his Son lacks something decisive: the *pain* of God.

Paul "decided to know nothing among you except Jesus Christ and him crucified" (1 Cor. 2:2). Everything hinges on the Christ of the cross. The fact of the cross is the axiom of theological thought. It is impossible to think about the gospel if we have the slightest hesitation on this point. We must determine to carry this theme throughout all the problems of theology without exception. This should also apply to the problem of the "essence" of God with which we are here concerned. *The essence of God can be comprehended only from the "word of the cross."* The pain of God is his "essence"—theology that is ashamed of this still belongs to the "theology of glory," *theologia gloriae*. The "theology of the cross," *theologia crucis*, is, strictly speaking, the theology which wonders most deeply at "pain as the essence of God."

In the gospel the primary words are "the Father causes his Son to die"; the secondary words are "the Father begets his Son." The secondary words prepare for the primary. In the gospel the final word is the *pain of God*. In trying to reveal his own pain to us as human beings, God communicates through human pain. To us the bitterest pain imaginable is that of a father allowing his son to suffer and die. Therefore God spoke his ultimate word, "God suffers pain," by using the father-son relationship. Thus the words "the Father begets the Son" are secondary to the primary words "the Father causes his Son to die." This is the theology of the cross. Any theology hesitating to make this point belongs to the theology of glory, no matter how eloquently it defends itself. Therefore we should not be absorbed in the mere words "the Father begets the Son." Our interest should be directed to "the Father causes the Son to die."

In classical Trinitarianism, not only a term such as "essence," but also the terms "beget" and "proceed" are full of problems. Luther wrote with insight as follows:

"This birth, therefore, is completely different from a human birth, and the procession (*Ausgang*) completely different from that of a human being. For a man, who is born of another man, has a different personality from his father, but also a different essence. He will not remain in the essence of his father, nor the father in the essence of his son. However, the Son, while being born of another personality, nevertheless remains in the essence of the Father, and the Father also remains in the essence of the Son. They are thus distinct in respect to their persons, but they remain one, undivided and inseparable essence. When a man proceeds from and is sent from another man, not only the personalities but also the essences are separate from and go far from the other. But here the Holy Spirit proceeds from the Father and the Son . . . and yet remains in the essence of the Father and the Son, though distinct in person. Thus, all three persons exist in one Godhead."[7]

With respect to the nature of the birth, a divergence also will be observed: "Again, human sonship involves temporal sequence in origin of father and son; whereas the begetting of the Son of God is eternal, and He is co-eternal with the Father. Once more, a human son is begotten in a state of partial development, and has to grow before he can attain to the full manhood of his father; whereas the Son of God possesses from all eternity the irreducible fulness of His Father's Godhead. Finally, a human begetting constitutes a passing beginning of sonship, and one which is subsequently to be regarded as a past event; whereas the generation of the Son and His Sonship are alike eternal and are coincident."[8] Again, the difference between "begetting" and "proceeding" is not clear. Augustine is content to think that the Holy Spirit should be pictured not as a being to be born, but as a being to be given.[9] It is still possible to ask why the subject who begets is called "father" instead of "mother."

In short, the word "beget"—as well as the word "proceed" —involves an imprecise and problematic concept. Had this word been primary for the truth about God there would have been extreme confusion and the church would have been perplexed. As long as we listen to the word of God as the gospel, the term "beget" never demands primary attention but serves the primary word, "the word of the cross." Consequently, the inexactness of this word will be endured, and the confusion arising from it will be mitigated.

> It is clear that in the personal circumstances of Paul's life, the "pain of God" was primary and "the Father begets the Son" was secondary. The apostle Paul experienced the pain of God most deeply. But Paul remained unmarried and did not know the experience of having a son. Paul would never have become the greatest apostle if "the Father begets the Son" had been primary. Yet Paul became the greatest apostle, although he lacked the condition enabling him to experience the secondary word, because the "pain of God" was primary.

Chapter Four

Service for the Pain of God

I

Our Lord Jesus Christ commanded: "If any man would come
after me, let him deny himself and *take up his cross* and follow
me" (Matt. 16:24), and "he who does not *take up his cross* and
follow me is not worthy of me" (Matt. 10:38). This is the absolute commandment and declaration. We must bear the cross to
serve the Lord of the cross.

The real meaning of the cross of the Lord is the pain of God.
To follow the Lord of the cross is to serve the pain of God. Thus,
to follow the Lord of the cross, bearing one's own cross, is to
serve the pain of God by suffering pain oneself. *Serve the pain of
God by your own pain*—this is the Lord's absolute commandment. "Those who do not serve the pain of God by their own pain
are not worthy of God's pain"—this is the absolute declaration.
What specifically does serving the pain of God through our pain
mean? Where can we find an example of this service to God? I
explored this question for a long time. Thanks be to God, he has
answered me. In Abraham he showed me an example of service
for the pain of God. Where else could I find a better answer! I
wish to discuss the truth found in Abraham.

It is most fitting that Abraham is called the "father of faith."
This phrase, however, does not do justice to Abraham's significance. In my opinion Abraham is the *father of service to God*, as
well as the father of faith. He is an example of what faith is; he is
also an example of what service to God is.

The great figure of Abraham is described three times: at his departure for Canaan in Genesis 12; in the oracle announcing the birth of his son in chapters 15 to 18; and at the offering of Isaac on Mount Moriah in chapter 22. I believe the first two references reveal Abraham chiefly as the father of faith, while the third depicts him mainly as the father of service to God. I am afraid the significance of the third scene has often been neglected. It is not that Abraham is not depicted as the father of faith in the third scene, but the emphasis is on his service to God rather than on his faith. Verses 12 and 18 would make this point clear. Thus I came to see Abraham on Mount Moriah in Genesis 22 as the father of service to God, and I saw an example of service for the pain of God.

God "tested Abraham" to see if he "fear[ed] God" (Gen. 22:1, 12), and Abraham "obeyed [his] voice" and served him. In what way did he serve God? God showed the way concretely in a commandment: "Take your son, your only son Isaac, whom you love, and go to the land of Moriah, and offer him there as a burnt offering upon one of the mountains of which I shall tell you" (vs. 2). And Abraham, obeying the command, "put forth his hand, and took the knife to slay his son." Just then God held his hand and showed him a ram to be offered instead of Isaac (vss. 12-13). In spite of God's help, Abraham felt as if he had already killed his son—that is, he did not "withhold" his only son from God (vs. 12). As a New Testament writer described penetratingly, Abraham received Isaac back as if "God was able to raise men even from the dead" (Heb. 11:19). When Abraham raised his knife to sacrifice Isaac, he felt he had already killed his son. Because of this act we "bow seven times at the name of Abraham, and for this act we bow seventy times" (Kierkegaard). O where else shall we find a man like Abraham? The eyes of anyone who witnessed the event on Mount Moriah would have frozen with horror. "From that day Abraham became an old man" (Kierkegaard).

What is the significance of Abraham's deed on Mount Moriah? It seems to me that the significance of this deed has not yet been fully known. (Even Kierkegaard's *Fear and Trembling* is no exception.)

Abraham served God by sacrificing his only beloved son: he served God by his own pain, for the bitterest pain man can suffer is to cause the death of his beloved son. Why then did God command Abraham to serve him by suffering pain? What sort of God is this whom Abraham served with pain? This God is the one who caused his own beloved Son to die, the God in pain, the Father of our Lord Jesus Christ. The service of God which the Lord commanded is serving pain with our own pain, bearing our own cross, and following the Lord of the cross. On Mount Moriah, Abraham left an example of service to God, thus becoming both the father of faith and the *father of service to God*. To serve the pain of God by his own pain—this is the significance of Abraham's act.

II

"Take up your cross and follow me." "Serve the pain of God through your own pain." Are these commands cruel? If we fail to understand their real intention, these commands may seem cruel. If we have insight into their purpose, however, we find that they are the means of our salvation. Let us seek the purpose of these commands.

The purpose of these commands is to *heal* our pain. Our pain is actually healed when it serves the pain of God. The Lord has promised that when we bear our cross for him and lose our life for him, we find our life (Matt. 16:25). Our wounds will be healed when they serve our Lord's wounds (1 Peter 2:24). How does this happen?

Our human pain is by itself dark, meaningless, and barren. Man's pain is the wrath of God. The wages of sin is death (Rom. 6:23) and "death is the wrath of God."[1] It is impossible to heal our pain, and we cannot be saved from it, since it is the reality of the wrath of God.

Yet God responded to this pain of ours in an astonishing way: he made it serve as testimony to *his own pain*. God could only reveal his pain to man through our own pain. God uses our pain as testimony to his. What then happens to our pain?

By serving as witness to the pain of God, our pain is transformed into light; it becomes meaningful and fruitful. By the pain

of God which overcomes his wrath, our pain, which had hitherto
been the reality of the wrath of God, ends in salvation from this
wrath. By serving the pain of God which is the glad news of
salvation, our pain ends in sharing this salvation. By serving him
through our pain, the pain of God rather saves and heals our own
pain. When the pain of God heals our pain, it already has changed
into love which has broken through the bounds of pain—"the love
rooted in the pain of God." By this love, whoever follows the
Lord, bearing his own cross and losing his life for Christ's sake,
will find life. Through our service in the pain of God, the wounds
of our Lord in turn heal our wounds, thus our pain can actually be
relieved by serving the pain of God. All kinds of pain experienced
in this world remain meaningless and fruitless as long as they do
not serve the pain of God. We must take care not to suffer human
pain in vain.

III

We must note carefully that even the very experience of pain
can exist as *sin*. Therefore only the pain of God as *forgiveness* of
sin can save us. To cause a loved one to suffer pain and die is for
us men the greatest pain imaginable. This is why God revealed his
pain through "the Father caused his Son to die." But for us this
sort of experience is made up of sin. Without discussing here the
fact that suffering and death are the result of sin, we must observe
that our pain at the suffering and death of a loved one is fundamentally the reality of sin. Why? Because we feel pain only when
a *loved one* suffers or dies. This kind of pain is self-centered and
particularistic. The more intense our love is, the more intense
our pain. Though we may spare some pain for those we do not
love so intensely, it is not as fervent. Between parent and child we
find the most intense love, and therefore the most intense pain.
Thus God decided to cause his Son to die. Yet with us human
beings, there is nothing so self-centered and particularistic as the
love between parent and child. Consequently, when our pain is
keenest, our sin works most greatly. Among us the intensity of
pain is found only through the medium of sin. How tragic this is!
Man's pain is therefore a most dreadful thing.

God used this dreadful reality of man's pain as a testimony to his own pain. It is only for this reason that God, who uses man's pain, is God in *pain*. God, who bears man's dreadful sin, could only be God in pain. We must ponder this most deeply. The pain of God can be communicated to us only through the medium of our sin.

When Jesus declared, "he who does not take his cross and follow me is not worthy of me" (Matt. 10:38), he also said, "He who loves father or mother more than me is not worthy of me; and he who loves son or daughter more than me is not worthy of me" (vs. 37). This announcement appears extremely harsh; yet it means our salvation. If we do not heed it—if parents indulge in their love for their children, and children indulge in their love for their parents—men will become completely indulgent to sin. Though parents suffer pain for their children, and children suffer pain for their parents, if their concern is centered on their own pain and their indulgence in it, they too are letting themselves drift into sin. This sort of love is self-centered and particularistic.

If we center our pain in the pain of God, until it is purified by his, our pain is saved from sinfulness for the first time. Using our pain to serve the pain of God means loving God more than we love our parents, our sons, our daughters. Only by this service are we fitted for Christ. It is unquestionably a great deed when a parent sends his child to suffer, but if his mind is completely absorbed by it, he is unworthy of Christ. Man becomes conformed to Christ when his concern is absorbed in the pain of God—when he serves the pain of God through his own pain. This is the way of salvation from sin. Our pain is sanctified when we serve the pain of God. Our pain becomes just and meaningful only as a testimony to the pain of God.

IV

Our pain should serve as testimony to the pain of God: in theological terms, there emerges between God and us an analogy (*analogia*) through the medium of pain. However, for theology, particularly evangelical theology, no concept raises so many problems as the term "analogy." This concept may become the "gate of the devil," for it is potentially fatal. According to a theology which insists on a motif of "opposition of principles" between God and man, the analogy of being (*analogia entis*) was invented by the antichrist and prevents people from becoming Catholics.[2] It is true that the "analogy" is even recognized within evangelical theology in a form of "analogy of faith" (*analogia fidei*). However, the basic meaning of "analogy" has been lost in the concept of "analogy of faith." It is not difficult to adopt a concept which has lost its basic meaning. In this case, the problem has not been solved, but dissolved; the problematical nature of the concept remains unsolved.

What is the problematic nature of the Catholic "analogy of being" which maintained its basic meaning? "Analogy" does not simply insist on the often superficially viewed continuity between God and man. Even in the Thomist and Catholic sense of the word, analogy is considered a continuity based upon the presupposition of difference or discontinuity between God and man. Analogy is, so to speak, "similarity in dissimilarity." The original purpose of the concept of analogy is to indicate the aspect of similarity, while the aspect of dissimilarity is merely a presupposition in order to speak of similarity. The purpose of the concept of analogy is thoroughly *positive*, and the "analogy of being" may be called "positive theology." It is not a mistake or overstatement to say that theology should become positive in order to accomplish its function; we should acknowledge this intention. When theology is driven by an impulse to dare to say something about God, it is not unreasonable for it to take a positive attitude. The concept of analogy aims to express itself in a "daring manner."

We should note, however, that it is *man* who "dares to speak," not God. Man can speak positively about God only through *his being as man*; hence the term "analogy of *being*." Here man's being serves positively. Indeed, the being of man works as witness and service to the being of God. But when do we find the guarantee that the being of man is *allowed* to serve the being of God? Where do we find guaranteed that such service is *valid*? Do not willfulness, illusion, and disobedience accompany service based on similarity? When we dare to speak with similarity as our medium, are we not making the mistake of ascribing to God what should not be ascribed to him? In short, man's *disobedience* is the unresolved problem of the analogy of being, for disobedience is part of man's *nature*. A paramount problem of the Catholic "analogy of being" is that it hurriedly sought the solution without thinking seriously about what was basic in human existence. Catholic analogy has been unable to solve the question of disobedience because it went no further than the analogy of being.

The only analogy which can solve the problem of disobedience, so helplessly entangled in every vanity of analogy, is the *analogy of pain* (*analogia doloris*). In the pain of God is his power which completely conquers the disobedience so deeply embedded in all human activities. In the analogy of pain, man's pain serves the pain of God, who completely conquers our willfulness, illusions, and disobedience. *God accepts our service by resolving our disobedience.* Thus man's pain serves the pain of God by receiving such *status* that it can never fall into disobedience. Here the concept of analogy is regarded as thoroughly soteriological. On the other hand, the Catholic analogy of being goes no further than the order of creation.

The "theology of the pain of God" dares to speak about the pain of God by means of the analogy of pain. This is service for the pain of God. But now our pain serves the pain of God while our disobedience is overcome by the pain of God whom we serve. Is there any other form of service for which we can be so thankful?

> There is another aspect to the analogy of pain: the position of the *Virgin Mary*. She is called the "mother of sorrows," *mater dolorosa* ("a sword will pierce through your own soul also," Luke 2:35). Although she was a true human mother, the pain she had to bear as a mother was inflicted by Jesus, the Son of God. Mary had to allow her beloved son Jesus to suffer and die. But Jesus was the *Son of God*. Thus the pain of God and human pain were joined in the person of Jesus. Mary was in the position of *uniting* the pain of God and human pain because of her son Jesus. Mary is the embodiment of the "analogy of pain." We must consider seriously the special significance attached to the Virgin Mary, though not, of course, in the Roman Catholic sense.
> We must also remember that God reveals himself as our

Father, the Father of mankind. Since he is the Father of mankind, he also experiences pain when we suffer. The Son, Jesus Christ, is not the only object of God's pain; all human beings are the objects of his pain as well. What an awesome thought this is! As the pain of God and human pain were united in the Virgin Mary, by the person of Jesus, so the pain of God and human pain are united by the reality of man. This also is an embodiment of the "analogy of pain."

Chapter Five

The Symbol of the Pain of God

I

Our task is to witness to the gospel. Before we can *talk about* the gospel, we must *hear* it and *see* it. Our words are empty if we talk about the gospel without hearing and seeing it. In witnessing to the gospel, we must first have ears to hear and eyes to see what God would reveal to us.

The gospel is the gospel of the cross. This means that God loves the objects of his wrath and that he, in his love, embraces men alienated from him. Theodosius Harnack insists that what is revealed in the cross is neither the wrath of God nor his love alone, but a *tertiary* (*tertium*) uniting the two.[1] Our ultimate task is to clarify this. Here theology begins to deal seriously with the matter of *content*. Such is the primary task of theology. Until now theology has concentrated on the matter of form, which is revelation, but now is the time to take a further step in dealing with its primary responsibility.

> Some theologians may argue that "revelation" is not merely a formal concept but one of content. This may be true only when a particular theological viewpoint is taken as a premise; but, to be impartial, "revelation" should still be regarded as a formal concept. In the Bible, revelation always indicates *"something* is revealed"; the form of revelation is always *governed* by the accompanying content. For instance, in Romans 1:17 and 3:21, "the righteousness of God is revealed"; in 1 John 4:9, "the love of God was made manifest," and so forth. The primary emphasis in the Bible is in this content and not in the concept of revela-

tion. If we are concerned only with the form and neglect the content, theology becomes cold and colorless. This theology has obviously departed far from such theology as that of the Apostle Paul.

II

When we search the Bible, we find in Jeremiah 31:20 the *pain of God*, the tertiary uniting the wrath of God and the love of God.

In our effort to witness to the gospel, we may be permitted to create a new concept most suitable for this witness, so long as there is no such concept already in existence. There is, for instance, the *homo-ousion* of Athanasius, and, of a slightly different type, Otto's "numinous." But should not this sort of thing be avoided as much as possible? Any term to form a new concept should be borrowed from the Bible if possible. But here we encounter difficulty. The definition of a new concept is required in witnessing to the gospel, because we are asked to clarify a point never fully grasped in previous understanding of the Bible. But this may never be met if we try to find a term in the Bible to express such a concept. It is therefore understandable that the creeds of the church, for instance, have to use terms not in the Bible. We, however, seek to find the necessary terms in the Bible if possible, and avoid the use of nonbiblical terms. Here lies a difficult dilemma. What we should do is give fresh meaning to a hitherto *overlooked* term in the Bible. This is what Forsyth calls a "new pronounciation." A new pronounciation no doubt—but the words are old.

"My heart is troubled" in Jeremiah 31:20 is an astonishing phrase, but it is no less astonishing that it has received so little attention until now. A good example of this neglect is found in the following words of the Old Testament scholar A. C. Welch.[2] According to him, the expression that God suffers pain is found only in Isaiah 63:9, and there the sense is obscure. Apparently Welch is ignorant of Jeremiah 31:20. This is indeed astonishing. (For an exegesis of Jeremiah 31:20, see the appendix of this book.) Isaiah 63:9 says that God suffers with suffering mankind, but this is quite different from the gospel of the cross—God's pain in loving sinful men. Jeremiah 31:20, however, literally agrees with the truth of the cross. No more appropriate words can be found to reveal the truth of the cross. Advocating the importance of this text is not a matter of choice for me, but a responsibility.

However, we cannot know directly what the pain of God is; we can know it only through *our own pain*. Our pain must witness to the pain of God by becoming the *symbol* of the pain of God. In his exposition of Jeremiah 31:20, Calvin says that pain does not properly belong to God (*proprie in Deum non competit*), but that God expresses his love in no other way (*non potest aliter exprimere*).[3] In these words of Calvin the essence of the "symbol" is expressed almost perfectly. The essence of the symbol lies in its inappropriateness (*non . . . proprie*) and in its inevitableness (*non . . . aliter*). Because of this "inappropriateness," man, essentially different from God, is required as a witness; because of this "inevitableness," God requires man of necessity.

> It is noteworthy that the pain of God is found in the Old Testament. According to A. B. Davidson, the truth of the New Testament is the "disembodied soul," while the truth of the Old Testament is symbolic truth, "soul with the body," "symbolical religion." The symbol is "material clothing." "Body" and "material" here mean *human truth*.[4]
>
> "Dostoevsky understood—at least strongly sensed—before anyone else that in religion, as in all life, unconditioned truth and unconditioned falsehood do not exist. He understood that there are highly conscious unconditioned signs, pointers, and symbols, though degree may differ. By rejecting the symbols of the ultimate being, Tolstoy's religious consciousness saw religion as something spiritual, without flesh and blood—a God separated from traditions, ceremonies, rites, and doctrines. Dostoevsky's religious consciousness was the highest ever seen in man: "a thought spoken is a falsehood." All thoughts of God, all truths of God conceived by men, are false. Men cannot speak the truth about God—but they cannot remain silent about him. Must they then utter falsehoods? No, man must speak in conditioned language, thereby approaching the truth, although never reaching it. He must be conscious, not of the falsity of language, but of its extreme conditionedness and relativity. Consciousness is the condition for all religious truth. Love unfolds all religious conditionedness and all the truth of symbols. We cannot love God without knowing him. We can only know and love God simultaneously. We can know only by loving, love only by knowing. The union of knowledge and love is one new religion, Dostoevsky's religion."[5]

The word "symbol" is derived from the Greek *symbolon*, the cognate noun of the verb *symballein*, "to unite." A symbol witnesses to divine truth by uniting human and divine truth. Man's pain becomes a symbol of the pain of God because God and man are united through the condition of pain.

Man's pain, however, is the reality of the *wrath* of God against sin, and is the result of man's *estrangement* from God.

> My anguish, my anguish! I writhe in pain!
> Oh, the walls of my heart!
> My heart is beating wildly;
> I cannot keep silent;
> for I hear the sound of the trumpet,
> the alarm of war.
> Disaster follows hard on disaster,
> the whole land is laid waste.
> Suddenly my tents are destroyed,
> my curtains in a moment. . . .
> I looked, and lo, the fruitful land was a desert,
> and all its cities were laid in ruins
> before the LORD, before his fierce anger.
>
> (*Jer.* 4:19-20, 26)
>
> What will you say when they set as head over you
> those whom you yourself have taught
> to be friends to you?
> Will not pangs take hold of you,
> like those of a woman in travail?
> And if you say in your heart,
> "Why have these things come upon me?"
> it is for the greatness of your iniquity
> that your skirts are lifted up,
> and you suffer violence.
>
> (*Jer.* 13:21-22)
>
> Her foes have become the head,
> her enemies prosper,
> because the LORD has made her suffer
> for the multitude of her transgressions;
> her children have gone away,
> captives before the foe. . . .
> "Is it nothing to you, all you who pass by?
> Look and see
> if there is any sorrow like my sorrow
> which was brought upon me,
> which the LORD inflicted
> on the day of his fierce anger."
>
> (*Lam.* 1:5, 12)

Consequently, the pain of man becomes the symbol of the pain of God, and God and man become united through pain, because this union takes place in *estrangement*. This union is assured by the pain of God loving the object of his wrath, embracing the estranged from God.

III

We have considered the "symbolization of pain" as an *act of testimony*. But it has yet another significance.

There are both believers and unbelievers among the men who are the objects of pain. Believers are conscious of being admitted into the pain of God and are aware that their own pain is a symbol of the pain of God. But unbelievers do not recognize their pain as a symbol of the pain of God; the fiercer their pain, the greater their estrangement, to the point of their complete separation. "The fifth angel poured his bowl on the throne of the beast, and its kingdom was in darkness; men gnawed their tongues in anguish and cursed the God of heaven for their pain and sores, and did not repent of their deeds" (Rev. 16:10-11).

> "To believers the symbol (consequently, reality) is an opportunity to find God, while to unbelievers it is an obstacle hiding God. Thus it has a dual function: giving light to some people, throwing others into darkness. It is important to understand this dual nature."[6]

In this connection, the attitude of believers toward unbelievers is of utmost importance. It must be the *symbolization of pain* as an *act of intercession*. Unbelievers can never be united to God as long as they are in their natural condition. Believers, though they have already been freed from the wrath of God, must share the pain of unbelievers, and thus help them to accept their pain as a symbol for God's pain in order to be united with God. Intercession is an act to unite with God those who are unable to be united by themselves. The love with which the pain of God embraces those estranged guarantees objectively that believers can perform acts of intercession. The believer can perform this intercessory act toward the unbeliever because the believer loves.

IV

The wrath of God means the estrangement of man from God, and man's pain reflects the reality of God's wrath. Although God's wrath exists, it is sometimes not actualized. In this case, a man, even though estranged from God, may live happily and die in peace (Job 12:6; 21:7-13, 23-24). Estranged from God, he has no point of contact with God. But when the wrath of God is actualized and man suffers pain, God and man are united through the pain, the symbol of the pain of God. "Blessed are those who mourn . . ."

> Does not the story of the rich man and Lazarus in Luke 16:19 ff. shed light on the above-discussed point? The rich man had received "good things," and Lazarus "evil things" (vs. 25), during their lifetimes, and the former fell into the place of separation from God (Hades) while the latter was united with God (in Abraham's bosom). Lazarus was united with God just because he had led a life full of pain, while the rich man was estranged from God just because he had led a happy life without suffering any pain. What was crucial in their fates was not good and evil, or faith and unbelief, but the happy life and the suffering life. (The picture of a rich man's life in verse 19 does not seem to portray evil, but simply the comfortable life of a wealthy man.) We should not read into this text a value judgment of good and evil, or faith and unbelief. The difficulty of the text may cause some to read into it a meaning not intended. I believe that the above-considered "symbolization of pain" removes this difficulty. Man (regardless of his goodness or his faith) is united with God by his pain; man (regardless of his evilness or unbelief) is severely estranged from God by his lack of pain. This interpretation is possible because the original meaning of "symbol" is "union" or "combination."
>
> It is written that the rich man was "in torment" in Hades (vs. 23). Could it not be, then, that he too, by the realization of his torments in Hades, the place of separation, saw from far off the symbol of the pain of God, and thus was received into union with him? Is this not the truth of Christ's "descending into hell," and the intention of the doctrine of universal salvation? But this is not our immediate problem.

Witness must be made to the pain of God. For this purpose man's pain must become a living symbol. Thus we seek to find

the wrath of God. The prophets before the Exile constantly sought
the wrath of God. From Amos to Ezekiel, they sought for the
manifestations of the wrath of God. Jeremiah, for instance,
suffered obloquy from the people because the wrath of God was
not revealed (Jer. 20:8). The prophets sought the wrath of God,
God's very wrath. This clarifies their difference from us. We do
not seek God's wrath itself; we seek God's wrath which creates
man's pain in order that we may witness to the pain of God. The
prophets sought the wrath of God; we seek the pain of God, which
heals our wounds caused by his wrath. When the pain of man
becomes the symbol of the pain of God and unites with the pain of
God, man's pain is in turn healed. What heals our wounds is the
love rooted in the pain of God. It is clear that by the manifestation
of his wrath, the pain of God is realized, and the love rooted in his
pain becomes a reality.

The gospel must always be preached. We must always bear in
our bodies the death of Jesus (2 Cor. 4:10). We must always
witness to the pain of God. Man's pain as a symbol must always
be on hand. We must never allow pain to leave us, even when
everybody else forgets his pain. Our very person must be in pain;
pain must be our *function*. "Jesus will be in agony even to the end
of the world. We must not sleep during that time."[7]

To become a symbol of the pain of God is to serve God. "Take
up your cross and follow me." In this service lies the promise of
salvation, for those who are united with God through their pain
are healed by the pain of God (1 Peter 2:24). "Whoever loses his
life for my sake will save it." That is why the pain of God becomes love rooted in the pain of God (Isa. 63:15). "Blessed are
those who mourn, for they shall be comforted."

> What can I say for you, to what compare you,
>   O daughter of Jerusalem?
> What can I liken to you, that I may comfort you,
>   O virgin daughter of Zion?
>   (*Lam.* 2:13)

Man's pain is difficult to heal when we cannot find in this
world comparisons or metaphors to describe it. A man in the
throes of death will not be comforted by the consoling words of
a living man. "The living do not possess true consoling words for

the dying. 'Let the dead bury the dead': it is only the dead who can really bury the dead. Survivors cannot judge, nor do they possess the art to comfort, the dead."[8] But because God is omnipotent, he can bestow a comparable pain on the incomparable pain of man. By this comparable and metaphorical pain of God, man's grievously difficult pain can be healed. To become a symbol of the pain of God is to heal the pain of man.

v

The concept "Servant of the Lord" (*Ebed Yahwe*) in Deutero-Isaiah throws great light on the "symbolization of pain" discussed above. There is general agreement that there are four "Servant of the Lord" passages: Isaiah 42:1-4; 49:1-6; 50:4-9; and 52:13–53:12. The last of these passages is of special importance for our present discussion.

There are three types of interpretations of the "Servant of the Lord." The first interprets him as the whole nation of Israel; the second, as a remnant of Israelites; and the third, as one individual.

> This second interpretation is comprised of two variations: one is the view of a few Israelites; the other is the ideal Israel. But the advocates of the "ideal Israel" theory think of the ideal Israel as established in a few Israelites, thus similar to the first theory. According to Skinner, the ideal Israelites are embodied in the experience of the "remnant," the "godly minority" who are "spiritually minded."[9] According to Davidson, they are represented by "an Israel within Israel."[10] Therefore the two views are really one.

Now there is reason for each of these three interpretations, but any one of them is incomplete by itself. The concept of the Servant of the Lord is "unusually elusive,"[11] and as Matthew Arnold once said, "It may be safely said that all these are meant, sometimes the one of them, sometimes the other."[12] Delitzsch envisions a "pyramid of the Servant of the Lord," with the base as the whole nation of Israel, the sides consisting of a few devout Israelites, and the apex formed by one individual; this is the most satisfactory among the interpretations.[13]

The Servant of the Lord definitely has some connection with the real Israel: he is called "Israel" (Isa. 49:3). The Servant being regarded as the actual Israel all through Deutero-Isaiah confirms

this view. The problem in the mind of the author of the Servant of
the Lord passages was the historic fact of the destruction of the
nation Israel. He also knew, from the traditions of the prophets,
that the downfall of Israel was caused by the wrath of God. The
destruction of the nation was due to God's wrath at her sins, and
dark, meaningless, and barren was her calamity. It was "inevitable" disaster, "involuntary" calamity.[14]

But the prophet, using this actual pain as "material,"[15] transformed it into a *redemptive calamity*, a symbol of the pain of God.
The downfall of Israel has become a symbol of the death of
Christ.[16] The actual pain was there waiting to be transformed and
explained by an act of symbolization. "The Songs of the Servant
are an explanation of the mystery of a suffering already realized."[17] Here the problem is the actual suffering of the actual
Israel.[18] But Israel as a whole was unaware of it and insensible
(Isa. 42:18-21, 24, 25). The actual pain was transformed into a
symbol of the pain of God by the few sensible Israelites.[19] Within
Israel were two aspects: the reality and its symbol.[20]

In this situation the *consciousness* of the few was decisive. We
must give careful attention to how the Old Testament scholars
emphasize the word "consciousness."[21] Phrases such as "my
servant shall prosper" (Isa. 52:13), "by his knowledge shall the
righteous one, my servant, make many to be accounted righteous"
(Isa. 52:11), signify this consciousness or insight. Symbolization
is a kind of insight; we must listen to it (Isa. 50:5). Symbolization is a prophetic act. Thus the "Servant of the Lord" is considered as a group of prophets. Plachte calls the acts of a prophet
"symbol-creation" (*prophetische Symbolschöpfung*)[22] This prophetic insight ultimately has an individualistic character.[23] On
the first page of his commentary on Jeremiah, Peake quotes from
F. W. H. Myers: "Desperate tides of whole great world's an-
guish/Forced thro' the channels of a single heart."

> A view that the "Servant of the Lord" is Jeremiah is interest-
> ing and suggestive. But as two or three scholars have pointed out,
> the "Servant of the Lord" is greater than Jeremiah, and should
> not be compared with him.[24] Jeremiah was surely the first man to
> see the pain of God. But he was not a "man of pain"; rather, as

the so-called "Confessions of Jeremiah" reveal (11:20; 12:3; 15:17-18; 18:21-23), he was a man of anger. This is quite natural, for Jeremiah saw the pain of God only in the final stage of his life; he had never been governed or guided by his pain. It was the "wrath of God" which governed him all through life. It is natural that a man commissioned to declare the wrath of God should become a man of wrath. "I think that the defects of his piety are mainly traceable to a single root: viz. an incomplete possession by the spirit of love."[25] The "Servant of the Lord" as a man of pain is certainly superior to Jeremiah as a man of wrath. At any rate, he was not Jeremiah.

Thus the "Servant of the Lord" implies a pyramid of three possible meanings: the actual Israel, a few Israelites, and some individual.

VI

The suffering of the Servant of the Lord, however, is only a symbol of redemptive suffering, not redemptive suffering itself. The suffering of the Servant is "figuratively" a sacrifice, an approach to redemptive suffering.[26] Even if Israel suffers for the Gentiles, this suffering cannot be redemptive so long as Israel has her own sins and her righteousness does not exceed that of the Gentiles.[27] And even though the few in Israel who are comparatively righteous bear the sin of the whole people by showing their suffering, as long as they themselves are not absolutely righteous, their suffering cannot be redemptive suffering. The same is true with individuals. In other words, the pain of the "Servant of the Lord" is a *symbol* for the pain of God. This Servant's pain was fulfilled through the pain of God in Jesus Christ.

The church inherited the pain of God and became the symbol of the pain of God. Each believer becomes the "Servant of the Lord." "To Jesus Christ belongs a unique Saviourhood—yet to be saved by Him means to be made saviours of men."[28] "The Servant is, in a transferred sense, a personification of the whole Christian community."[29] What Israel could do only imperfectly, the church must do better. This can be accomplished by a development from the nationalistic particularity of Israel into the world-wide universality of the church.[30] The concept of the "Servant of the Lord" in the Old Testament moves from the community to the individual; in the New Testament it moves from the individual to the community.[31] Thus Israel and the church serve the mid-point of Jesus Christ. Israel is the symbol of a Savior who is to come; the church is the symbol of the Savior who has come. Israel prophesied the symbol of the pain of God, while the church witnessed to the symbol of the pain of God. Here the Israel which corresponds to the church is the "few" of the second theory mentioned above. What corresponds to Israel as a whole is the nations, the whole world, with the church in its midst. The acts of intercession—"the symbolization of pain"—always have unbelievers as the objective. The world is the object of God's promise through the church.

Isaiah's Servant of the Lord cannot be identified directly with Christ. This concept is definitely confined to the historical situation of Israel. This historicity is characteristic of a symbol. A symbol emerges to indicate transcendence while retaining the historical characteristics of reality.

To be conscious of its symbolical nature means to receive meaning from that to which it points, without claiming its own historical value of reality. When this symbolism is lost, even the deepest and most precious things of men fall away from the truth. Judaism fatally believes that the "Servant of the Lord" means Jews in the world today and does not take the Servant as a symbol of the pain of God in Christ.[32] It is for this reason that Judaism, in spite of all the vigor and volume of its assertions, bears little fruit and carries no persuasion in the world. Man's pain, no matter how great it is, remains meaningless and barren unless it becomes the symbol of the pain of God.

The "Servant of the Lord" renders service to God's glory as his *servant*. "You are my servant, Israel, in whom I will be glorified" (Isa. 49:3). "The absolute and holy God demands the mortal man in order for God's glory to be revealed."[33] Thus the witnesses become inevitably a symbol. The quality of the witness is determined by the consciousness of man's *symbolic* nature. The moment a man loses this consciousness, he immediately loses the status of his being a witness and begins to seek his own glory. This symbolic nature is therefore fundamental for a proper understanding of the "Servant of the Lord." Generally speaking, I am afraid that Old Testament scholarship does not have a sufficient comprehension of this matter. Is it not superficial to link the interpretation of the Servant as "individual" directly to the intention of Jesus Christ? Is there a clear comprehension of the *transcendent* nature of Christ as symbolized by the "Servant"? The transcendent nature of that which is symbolized determines its symbolical quality.

One of the striking characteristics of the "Servant of the Lord" is his *silence* under sufferings (Isa. 53:7-9; 42:3). The redemptive suffering is borne only in silence. And the "Servant of the Lord" was able to endure this unbearable suffering because he discerned God's will hidden in his suffering (52:13). He was able to withstand this tragedy because he knew it was God's will.[34]

By serving God's pain, the pain of the "servant," though barren by itself, becomes fruitful and enters into God's glory. "In contrast to human experience God reveals in His Servant that suffering is fruitful, that sacrifice is practical. Pain, in God's service, shall lead to glory."[35] He conquers the world and becomes its light because of the truth of pain (52:10-13; 42:1-4; 49:6).

The truth of pain as redemptive suffering is the "highest and holiest" reality of all. The attitude of the human race toward pain determines its rate of progress.[36] While scores of nations died out, Israel alone maintained its imperishable significance because of its distinct understanding of the truth of pain.

The distinctive characteristics of a nation are to be found in its self-assertiveness. But when this self-assertiveness becomes overweening, it becomes antagonistic toward other nations and is unable to persuade or include them. Even Israel was no exception to this when she was a wealthy and strong nation in the days of David and Solomon. But Israel underwent a powerful change because of her national disaster in the sixth century B.C.: she was transformed from a self-assertive nation into a self-sacrificing "church." Thus Israel finally was able to become a spiritual leader. From this point of view, we may say that Israel's history since her formation existed for the sake of the sixth century B.C.

The days of the "decline and fall" of Israel were the days of the "flourishing of heaven and earth."[37] "If Israel had had no religion of Yahweh and no exile, its history would have been no different from that of Persia and Damascus."[38] Here lies the wisdom of history. What can we learn from this?

Are we to suppose that Israel was the only country permitted to become a symbol of the pain of God? Are we not allowed to follow the same road? Should we not make every effort to walk the path of the "Servant of the Lord"? For, as J. M. Powis Smith said, "His admirers then, as now, were probably many; his followers, few." He also says of the "Servant of the Lord" concept: "Our 100% Americanism shudders in terror before such an idea as this."[39] What should we say when we hear such a frank confession?

In this chapter we have considered the symbol of the pain of God. We recall that the word "symbol" means "combination" in its original Greek sense. The transformation of our pain into a symbol of the pain of God signifies our unity with God through pain. But what does this union of God and man imply? It is a mystical condition, *unio mystica*. It is clear, then, that the mystical is contained in the symbolical concept. We shall consider this in the next chapter.

Chapter Six

The Mysticism of Pain

I

What is implied in the following passages? "Do you not know that all of us who have been baptized into Christ Jesus were baptized into his death? We were buried therefore with him by baptism into death . . ." (Rom. 6:3-4). "For if we have been united with him in a death like his . . ." (vs. 5). ". . . our old self was crucified with him . . ." (vs. 6). "But if we have died with Christ . . ." (vs. 8). "I have been crucified with Christ . . ." (Gal. 2:20). "And those who belong to Christ Jesus have crucified the flesh with its passions and desires" (Gal. 5:24). ". . . we share abundantly in Christ's sufferings . . ." (2 Cor. 1:5). ". . . share his sufferings, becoming like him in death . . ." (Phil. 3:10). ". . . you share Christ's sufferings . . ." (1 Peter 4:13). ". . . Christ also suffered for you, leaving you an example, that you should follow in his steps" (1 Peter 2:21). "By his wounds have you been healed" (vs. 24).

I am dissolved in the pain of God and become one with him in pain. This is what is actually revealed in these passages. In Luther's word, it is *condolore*,[1] "to suffer together" in the pain of God.

But such expressions as "being dissolved in" and "being at one with" are mystical in their connotation. Luther says concerning Romans 6:5: "to become one with him in his death means to be buried in a "mystical death," *in mysticam mortem*.[2] However, this is not ordinary mysticism, but a thoroughgoing "mysticism of the pain of God."

"No adequate explanation can be given about such phrases as 'to die and be buried with Christ', or 'to live in Christ' without using mystical terms."[3] The attitude of faith is: "What we are accustomed to calling 'mystical' . . . is to a large extent nothing else than self-evident and natural occurrences of devotion, and the deepened and renewed religious inner life itself."[4]

When I am dissolved in the pain of God and become one with him in pain, it is pure joy, and there can be no greater happiness for me. In the pain of God my pain is healed, my old self dies; I become God's obedient servant and am resurrected into a new life. This happens because the pain of God is love rooted in the pain of God.

The above-cited passages are found in the following context because of God's love: "We were buried therefore with him by baptism into death, so that as Christ was raised from the dead by the glory of the Father, we too might walk in *newness of life*" (Rom. 6:4). "For if we have been united with him in a death like his, we shall certainly be united with him in *a resurrection like his*" (vs. 5). "We know that our old self was crucified with him so that *the sinful body might be destroyed,* and we might no longer be enslaved to sin" (vs. 6). "But if we have died with Christ, we believe that *we shall also live* with him" (vs. 8). "I have been crucified with Christ; it is no longer I who live, but Christ who *lives* in me . . ." (Gal. 2:20). "For as we share abundantly in Christ's sufferings, so through Christ we share abundantly *in comfort* too" (2 Cor. 1:5). ". . . that I may know him and the power of his resurrection, and may share his sufferings, becoming like him in his death . . ." (Phil. 3:10). "But *rejoice* in so far as you share Christ's sufferings . . ." (1 Peter 4:13).

Just as the "pain" of God witnesses to the cross of Christ, so "love" rooted in the pain of God witnesses to the *Holy Spirit.* (In Romans 15:30 we find the expression "the love of the Spirit.") In the New Testament the mysticism of Christ is linked with the mysticism of the Spirit (e.g., in 2 Cor. 3:18), and this corresponds to the link between the pain of God and love rooted in the pain of God. But we are now concerned with the mysticism of Christ, the mysticism of pain.

II

If we were to describe merely our own experience of the mysticism of pain, I ought to lay down my pen. Such a description would only further obscure the matter. For being in the mystical state means, as the original word implies, to be silent and sink into its depths. The truly mystical condition is found not where men talk glibly about it, but where they are silent. Silence alone is its appropriate domain.

But what concerns us most is the problem of the theology of the pain of God. Theology is a most precise form of reflection. Therefore, in the question of mysticism of pain, I cannot be content to simply describe an experience of it. As we reflect precisely on the condition experienced, we must guard ourselves from being sidetracked. According to Hilty, "Christianity is nothing but sound mysticism." The following discussion aims at achieving this "soundness."

Our reflection should be guided by the principle that this mysticism is strictly the mysticism of the *pain of God*. We should also note that the mysticism of the pain of God is strictly *mysticism*. The pain of God distinguishes our mysticism from all other mysticisms, but our mysticism must retain the distinctive quality common to all mysticisms. Thus our reflections have a twofold task: on the one hand, to retain the distinctive quality of mysticism; on the other, to maintain the principle which distinguishes it from all others. Only by fulfilling these two tasks simultaneously can we secure a "sound mysticism." Thus our reflections cannot simply be mere reflections: they must be veritable descriptions of the mystical condition. Let us proceed by reflecting as we describe and describing as we reflect.

The first characteristic of mysticism is its immediacy. Phrases such as "to be dissolved in," "to become one with," express this immediacy. This characteristic is indispensable to mysticism: the mysticism of pain is no exception. Without this quality, mysticism does not exist. This is the reason for my previous statement: "I am *dissolved* in the pain of God and *become one* with him in pain."

But from the standpoint of the gospel, the pain of God, we noted that this immediacy must be *rejected* before anything else. For "immediacy" rejects the pain of God and makes the death of Christ in vain; it makes the *im-mediate* (*un-mittelbar*) possible without the Mediator. Mysticism boldly expresses immediacy. It is no accident that liberal theology, which denies emphatically the pain of God, is considered mystical (as in Emil Brunner's *Mysticism and the World*). Therefore, immediacy, the first characteristic of mysticism, is a hotbed for unsoundness.

Here we face a most difficult problem. Our aim is to secure a sound mysticism. As long as it is mysticism, this immediacy must be retained. But, theologically speaking, this immediacy is unsound. How then can we secure a "sound mysticism"? This is indeed a difficult problem, yet a sound mysticism must overcome it. This is possible because our mysticism is a "mysticism of pain."

The pain of God exists by the denial of immediacy. Yet we are dissolved into the pain of God and we are at one with him in this pain. Thus, in the mysticism of pain, *we become immediately at one with God who denies immediacy*. The pain of God continues to deny immediacy, and yet we are one with this pain of God which denies immediacy. This is the only way we can establish a "sound mysticism." As long as we are one with the pain of God, the characteristic of *mysticism* can be retained. This mysticism remains sound inasmuch as the pain of God denies immediacy, even when we are united with him.

Viewed from another perspective, unsoundness implies disobedience. A mysticism based on immediacy cannot free itself from disobedience. But the gospel, the pain of God, is his grace which completely conquers all our disobedience. Consequently, in the mysticism of pain, the disobedience of mysticism is completely resolved, yet the characteristic of mysticism is maintained. In theological terms, we may say that mysticism is based on the doctrine of justification. The inner relationship between mysticism and justification is suggested by Paul in Galatians 2:20. In mystical terms he says, "I have been crucified with Christ; it is no longer I who live, but Christ who lives in me," and immediately follows with terms of justification: "the life I now live in the flesh I live by faith in the Son of God." The progression from justification to mysticism is inevitable. A doctrine of justification which does not develop into mysticism lacks power. Mysticism based on justification is the first requisite for the mysticism of the pain of God as a sound mysticism.

> Dr. Shogo Yamaya clearly explains the necessary relationship between justification and mysticism in *The Theology of Paul*: "Paul's theology is not divided into two individual parts: justification and mysticism. It starts from his experience and develops as one unified body of thought."[5] Otto defines the characteristic of New Testament mysticism: "it is completely related to the doctrine of grace . . . this relationship with the experience of grace is peculiar to Christian mysticism (and to this extent, such mysticism is Christian. Everything else is a heathen mysticism)."[6] According to Otto, the mystical expressions in the New Testament are simply the "other side" (*Kehrseite*) of the expression of the doctrine of grace.

III

The second characteristic of mysticism is expressed by Augustine as "to enjoy God" (*fruitio Dei*). I implied this in my earlier statement: "When I am dissolved in the pain of God and become one with him in pain, it is pure joy, and there can be no greater happiness for me." This is perfectly true. "But rejoice in so far as you share Christ's sufferings . . ." (1 Peter 4:13). "For as we share abundantly in Christ's sufferings, so through Christ we share abundantly in comfort too" (2 Cor. 1:5). Our fellowship with Christ's suffering becomes our joy and comfort: this is because the pain of God is immediately love rooted in his pain. From the standpoint of the gospel, namely, the pain of God, this "enjoyment of God" must be *denied*. Sin is loving oneself (2 Tim. 3:2). The pain of God is the forgiveness of this sin. When one's sins are forgiven and he enters the pain of God, he must hate himself (Luke 14:26; John 12:25). By "enjoying God" one begins to love oneself because he is in a state of enjoying himself. From the standpoint of the pain of God, therefore, the "enjoyment of God" must be denied.

One of Luther's greatest contributions was the proclamation of this truth. "Even in his relationship with God, man seeks himself in his self-searching love."[7] "By the desire of the flesh man loves himself above everything, even above God."[8] "To love God is to hate oneself." "The righteous man, after all, condemns himself." "To love is to hate and condemn oneself, to seek disaster for oneself, and to follow the words of Christ: 'He who hates his life in this world shall keep it unto life eternal' (John 12:25)."[9]

Here again we encounter a difficult problem. To secure a "sound mysticism," the "enjoying of God" must be given its proper place; while its accompanying problems must be solved completely, this solution is possible through a thorough understanding of the mysticism of pain.

The pain of God takes place because of his will to forgive sin, namely, self-seeking. Our joy, pleasure, and happiness, which accompany the "enjoyment of God," are but sins of self-seeking. The pain of God is his will to forgive these sins *completely*. How then is the completeness of the forgiveness of sin revealed to us?

When we find ourselves in the pain of God, we become aware of our own sin and begin to hate ourselves. Yet we know that God loves us intently. This love of God is so intent that it *surpasses*, and even *forgets*, the pain of God. The development of the pain of God into the love rooted in his pain reveals its real nature. The pain of God demands that we hate ourselves, but love rooted in the pain of God envelops us so completely that we cannot even hate ourselves any longer. This is the love of "God who richly furnishes us with everything to enjoy" (1 Tim. 6:17). Because God loves us so deeply he gives us an object for our enjoyment: himself. It is here that the mysticism of "enjoying God" is established.

However, the love of God remains as the true condition of his pain. Because this pain is God's, he develops it into his love. Our sin of enjoying God is forgiven by the pain of God, which continues to suffer for us and gives us an object of our enjoyment.

We should never forget to "hate ourselves" even in the very moment of our enjoyment of God, choked by tears at the thought of our being loved so surpassingly by him.

Thus the pain of God disposes of all the sin clinging to our enjoyment and God offers himself as the object of our enjoyment. Here the mysticism of "enjoying God" becomes a "sound mysticism."

> Luther asks, "Is it reasonable for Christ's body to live in joy while his head is suffering at its wounds?" He adds that in the gospel "we continually dance for joy."[10]

IV

The third characteristic of mysticism is its *ethical nature*. This is why mysticism insists that self-seeking must be negated by being "put off." In the New Testament, the mythical ethic is indicated in the following words: "And those who belong to Christ Jesus have crucified the flesh with its passions and desires" (Gal. 5:24). "For he who has died is free from sin" (Rom. 6:7). "Since therefore Christ suffered in the flesh, arm yourselves with the same thought, for whoever has suffered in the flesh has ceased from sin . . ." (1 Peter 4:1). When we are dissolved in the pain of God and become one with him, the lusts and desires of the flesh eventually lose their power. The most effective method to destroy sin is to constantly lay the pain of God on ourselves. It is said that Zinzendorf, in order to enable his congregation to resist lust, urged them to "let themselves become cold and dead like stone by the deathly cold corpse."[11] Because the pain of God is love rooted in his pain, the mysticism of the cross creates power for sanctification. This love of God produces ethical sanctification in harmony with the order of the Holy Spirit. Mysticism which has justification as its background produces ethical energy—this is our mysticism.

However, for ethical mysticism to become a "sound mysticism," a more precise reflection is necessary. Generally speaking, one of the characteristics of mysticism is its insistence that it is "complete in itself." Mysticism is apt to be complacent, assuming it is complete; this is why mysticism usually ends in contemplative quietism. But the situation worsens when mysticism with ethical character insists that it is complete in itself. For when ethical sanctification is complacent in its achievement, the grace of God for the forgiveness of sins is unnecessary. For even though grace is taken as a premise or in anticipation, the principle of "grace alone" is denied and a Pelagian position of "grace and ethics" emerges. Indispensable as is ethical sanctification to true mysticism, if it is self-sufficient, the mysticism will become unsound. For mysticism to be sound, ethical santification should always admit its incompleteness. Because of this incompleteness and imperfection, we can only rely on the cross of Christ in the process of our sanctification.

"Grace and ethics" exist in the axiom of "grace alone," and the love of God at the place of the pain of God; the truth we have just discussed is reflected in these expressions. Paul expresses it perfectly in Galatians 2:20 and Philippians 3:12. Luther said, "Always justified, but always a sinner," *Semper iustus, semper peccator*. We should go one step further and say, "Sanctified but still a sinner."

When we are dissolved in and become one with the pain of God, our sin certainly loses its power. However, it is really tragic that our sin is so strong it may cast aside the pain of God and become demonic. Augustine said, "Sin rebels, yet is dead," *rebellat et mortuum*.[12] The reverse may be true: "Sin is dead, yet rebels." A reality in the life of sinners is that sin which should be dead still rebels. What are we to do in the face of this reality? We should gaze at the cross of Christ, which is the pain of God.

Since even the mysticism of pain is defeated in the face of sin, we have only the pain of God on which to rely. When ethical mysticism shipwrecks, it must be saved by a doctrine of justification. The mysticism which seeks its final salvation in a doctrine of justification is truly a "sound mysticism." *The pain of God, while uniting God and man mystically, continues to forgive and embrace the sin which betrays and breaks this union.* Self-complete mysticism is not the pain of God, but only an immediate love of God, which we discussed earlier.

> At this point we must carefully distinguish between what has been historically known as the "mysticism of suffering," *Leidensmystik, Passionsmystik*, and our "mysticism of pain." The mysticism of suffering is a peculiar experience or idea that flourished in Christian thought toward the end of the Middle Ages, with Bernard of Clairvaux as its representative figure. Today we must

listen carefully to this thought and heed its motif. However, we cannot accept wholeheartedly this mysticism of suffering, for the marks of a "sound mysticism" are lacking in its thought. In the first place, immediacy is affirmed without reflection; second, there is a tendency toward indulging in the enjoyment of God without reflection; third, there is room for merit-seeking thoughts. In short, we can detect the unsoundness of this type of mysticism, and therefore cannot endorse this point of view in its entirety. Thus we use the particular term "mysticism of pain," *Schmerzes-mystik*, to distinguish it from the mysticism of suffering.

v

In the chapter "Service for the Pain of God" we noted that we should serve the pain of God through *our own pain*. Now this truth must be applied to our own situation in regard to the mysticism of pain. The phrase "service for the pain of God" already contains within itself a seed of the mystical. When this seed develops, the practical application of the mysticism of pain will be made possible.

In order that the mysticism of pain—our being dissolved in the pain of God and our becoming one with him—may become concrete, *our own pain* must be used as its instrument.

We become united with the pain of God through our pain, and we are united with God through the joined pains. "I must add my wounds to his, and join myself to him."[13]

It is understandable that the Epistles of Peter, the most practical writings in the New Testament, deal most clearly with real-life situations. "For to this you have been called, because Christ also suffered for you, leaving you an example, that you should follow in his steps. . . . By his wounds you have been healed" (1 Peter 2:21, 24). "Since therefore Christ suffered in the flesh, arm yourselves with the same thought, for whoever has suffered in the flesh has ceased from sin . . ." (4:1).

> "I must suffer. My suffering must become the channel through which grace enters to transform my life. Now since Jesus Christ endured all the evils we deserve, suffering has become a point of similarity, a point of union between God and man. This is the only point of union in our world today. God can visit the human soul because of suffering. In his love God redeems the suffering

of sinners and unites it with his. Borne by Jesus Christ, my suffering receives the purifying and renewing power which comes only
from God."[14]

"To live in Christ is to participate in his suffering and be
received into his glory. He is our example, and he does not
exempt us from our own suffering because he himself suffered.
However, he offered us the means to make our own suffering
fruitful."[15]

In this practical aspect, mysticism for the first time can be
linked with ethics. ". . . for whoever has suffered in the flesh has
ceased from sin, so as to live for the rest of the time in the flesh no
longer by human passions but by the will of God" (1 Peter 4:1-2).

"Through suffering we strive to conquer the threefold wickedness within us of the emotion, the mind, and the will. By suffering we strive to free our hearts from the soiled, the mean, and
the degrading, and in their place restore the love of God."[16]

In such a case as this, our suffering must be very *realistic*.

"He [Pascal] understood that sickness, which weakens the body
and consequently, sensual desire, is the natural state of the
Christian. . . . He wore an iron belt studded with spikes pointing
in against his flesh. When a vain thought came to him, he struck
the belt with his elbow to increase the pressure of the spikes. He
denied himself all that would delight the senses. . . . His meticu-
lousness on this matter of purity is incredible. Even the most
pious saints were amazed. . . . In his letter to Mme. Périer, he
mentioned that to betroth her daughter in marriage would be,
in the words of the hermits of Port-Royal, to cause the married
couple to commit deicide."[17]

Our pain becomes healed, redeemed, and meaningful only when
it leads to unity with the pain of God. Our wounds are healed by
our Lord's wounds (1 Peter 2:24). Our only desire is to become
one in pain with God. Because of this desire we will seek and long
for our pain.

Our pain defeats us, and we fear it is because we regard it as an
inevitable disaster falling upon us from *outside* us. As long as we
try to escape it, we cannot resolve it. We can conquer it only when
we seek it within ourselves and long for it. We can strengthen
ourselves when we earnestly seek and desire pain to be part of our

nature. We are delivered from the fear of pain by setting our hearts upon pain. "There is no fear in love, but perfect love casts our fear" (1 John 4:18).

> "While our suffering is depressing when we accept it as the inevitable, his suffering, which is born of love, produces power and life."[18]

In an earlier chapter, "Pain as the Essence of God," we saw that pain was "fitting" to God (Heb. 2:10), and was his essence. Because of this, God's glory abounds through pain.

> Rich wounds, yet visible above
> In beauty glorified.

For those who follow the Lord, in beauty glorified by his wounds, pain becomes strengthening. We can truly overcome our suffering by recognizing it as our nature. More forcefully speaking, we must *become* suffering. To overcome death is to die before our physical death.

There are two ways to render service to the pain of God. The first is to let our *loved ones* suffer and die. The second is for *us* to suffer and die. The first witnesses to the "pain of *God*," the second to the "*pain* of God."

In accordance with these two ways of service to the pain of God, the mysticism of pain has two ways of practical application. First, we experience pain when we let our loved one suffer and die; second, we experience it when we suffer and die. In the above discussion we examined only the second way. But the truth we perceived above can apply equally to the first way. In the second way we become one with the "*pain* of God," whereas in the first we become one with the "pain of *God*." The "*pain* of God" refers to God the Son entering pain and dying; the "pain of *God*" refers to God the Father letting his only beloved Son suffer and die. We are united with the pain of *God* by experiencing the pain of letting our loved one suffer. Our pain is resolved and our wounds are healed when God and we are united in pain and his wounds with ours. The healing of our wounds is related to the resolving of the pain of our loved ones, whom we allowed to suffer. Because the pain of God is love rooted in his pain, the suffering of our loved

ones will be transformed from darkness to light, to meaningful
suffering. Thus we pray that our loved ones may be delivered from
pain.

The general truth discussed earlier in connection with the
mysticism of pain can be applied to the pain of the first way.
(There will be further discussion of the first method in the next
chapter, "The Pain of God and Ethics.")

VI

To live in the pain of God is to *hate oneself*. But how is it
possible to hate oneself?

We need to examine the followers of the so-called "mysticism
of suffering" of the Middle Ages. They passionately desired union
with Christ through pain, and tried to practice "self-renunciation"
as their discipline. To renounce oneself is to hate oneself. However, their very self-hatred caused *complacency*. They became
masochistic. Thus ascetic practices accompanied the "mysticism
of suffering." Thus the "mysticism of suffering" turned into what
Karl Holl has called *ein frommes Spiel*, "a pious play."

What caused this? Their self-hated was a result of their *inner
will power*. Man can use this inner will power in any way for his
own pleasure. Man's inner will power may seem to be opposed to
self-indulgence, but as long as it is inner, it is potentially selfish.
Indeed in such cases self-enjoyment gives the impression of refinement. Compared with decadent pleasure, mystical pleasure is
stronger and far more lasting. Even when carnal pleasure de-
creases and burns itself out, spiritual pleasure may burn steadily
and strongly. But to turn from carnal to spiritual pleasure is but
an exchange of tastes; it is still hedonistic. Though it may be
called "pious," it still remains a "play." Thus we concluded earlier
that the "mysticism of suffering" is an unsound mysticism.

The self-hatred in the mysticism of pain must be of a completely different kind. How is it possible to hate oneself truly? One
must use some sort of medium. So long as a person hates himself,
the self that hates is the same as the self that is hated, and
remains within. It is impossible to wound one's body by simply
using one's body. Even such a medium as one's inner will power

cannot injure oneself. Whatever one can handle by himself is a *means*, not a medium.

Only something *outside* the self, which one cannot command, can really injure the self. In order to injure one's body, a medium of a completely different nature, such as a stone, must be used. It must be different (*Heterothese*) but not antithetical (*Antithese*). What then is this stone which is absolutely different from us? It represents the broken order of creation, the reality of the *wrath of God*. We cannot deal with this reality by our own self-will. The wrath of God alone cause *suffering* which can wound us. The sin of self-loving ceases only when we receive this suffering physically. ". . . whoever has suffered in the flesh has ceased from sin . . ." (1 Peter 4:1). The heart which seeks such suffering has truly repented and hates itself. Luther calls this "a heart that loves judgment."

To hate oneself through the medium of the wrath of God is to live in the *pain* of God. This is unsearchable grace. For the wrath of God is used as the medium of the pain of God for our *salvation*, although it basically means our destruction. This is possible because the pain of God has already overcome the wrath of God. Through this grace a path is prepared on which we can walk with amazing strides. What amazing grace it is that the wrath of God, which should have wounded and weakened us, becomes the medium of the pain of God which heals and strengthens us. Certainly the wrath of God is outside of our control, but it is the proof of our conquered and resolved reality when used as a medium. The reality of the wrath of God is already conquered as long as we seek it. Judgment is no longer an object of fear for "a heart that loves judgment." "In this is love perfected with us, that we may have confidence for the day of judgment . . ." (1 John 4:17).

But this never implies the substitution of means for medium, as in the "mysticism of suffering." Means can be controlled by man's will, but medium—the reality of the wrath of God—is controlled not by man's power, but by the power of the *pain of God* which has overcome his wrath. The broken order of creation can be transformed from darkness into light by the power of the order of reconciliation, and then serve in the order of sanctification. When the wrath of God is mediated by the pain of God, it is absorbed in love rooted in the pain of God. ". . . if by the Spirit you put to death the deeds of the body you will live" (Rom. 8:13). The reality of the wrath of God must be the medium which puts an end to carnal deeds. The broken order of creation becomes the medium for the order of sanctification by the Holy Spirit.

When Jesus commanded us to hate ourselves, he also commanded us to hate our parents, wives, children, brothers, and sisters (Luke 14:26). Here the practical application of the mysticism of pain reaches its final stage. These persons are extensions of our own flesh. If there is danger that "hating oneself" should become idealized, playacting, the pain arising in persons who are extensions of our flesh serves as a medium for real hatred of oneself. Even when one's own pain is idealized, the pain of these persons prevents this idealization and becomes a "stone" to us. These words of Jesus are certainly piercing.

Chapter Seven

The Pain of God and Ethics

I

A true ethic is possible only when love is intense. In the commandment "You shall love your neighbor as yourself," what is affirmed is not self-love as the premise of love for neighbor, but rather the *intensity* which accompanies self-love. Self-love must always be denied. As Luther said, "To love means to hate and condemn oneself" (*Est enim diligere seipsum odisse*).[1] However, the love for your neighbor must be intense. This intensity is truly displayed in self-love. Therefore the great commandment means: "You shall love your neighbor as intensely as you love yourself."

Paul says, "Rejoice with those who rejoice, weep with those who weep" (Rom. 12:15). In every age, joy and pain are intertwined. There are periods in time, however, when joy is stronger than pain, and other periods when pain is stronger than joy. The former may be called "times of joy," the latter, "times of pain." The present is an age of pain. If our age is not to be called a "time of pain," for what period of history can the term be appropriate? As an ethic peculiar to the present age, the "ethic of pain," *Schmerzesethik*, must make its features clear. To "rejoice with those who rejoice" is certainly difficult, but it is no less difficult to "weep with those who weep." How often our sympathy and thoughtfulness, as Kierkegaard remarks, are nothing but curiosity under another name! Though we assume a pained appearance and say we are sympathizing with our neighbor's pain, actually we only want to stare curiously at him in his pain. If any sin is worthy of death, surely this is.

A true ethic is possible only when pain is intense. This characterizes the ethic of our age—the age of pain. Paul says, ". . . I have great sorrow and unceasing anguish in my heart" (Rom. 9:2). Luther comments on it as follows: "This passage shows clearly that love proves itself not so much in sweetness and delight, but in very great sorrow and bitterness. Indeed, it finds delight and sweetness in bitterness and sorrow, because it takes upon itself the misery and suffering of others. Thus Christ was aflame with love in the very great agony of his death."[2] The mark of a true ethic must be sought in the intensity of pain.

The next question is, How does the ethic of pain become actually possible? If you seek an ethic like this only within man's powers, you are seeking an impossibility. Truly to weep with those who weep, to feel another's pain as intensely as one does his own, is *psychologically* impossible. It must be concluded, therefore, that a principle like the "universal love" of Mo Ti is fanciful idealism. No immanental ethic can realize the ethic of pain.

The ethic of pain can be realized only through the *pain of God.* We can give to a suffering neighbor our love with an intensity equal to what we feel in our own pain only when we and that neighbor rest in the pain of God. That is, when we are both "of the same body . . . in Christ" (Eph. 3:6). Love for our neighbor becomes real for the first time when we walk in the way which God has shown us. Since we and our suffering neighbor are joined together when we are both embraced in the pain of God, we can feel our neighbor's pain as intensely as our own.

> Even if my neighbor and I share pain as human beings, there can be no ethic of pain unless it is joined with the pain of God. "There was a man lying near me who was dying. He had a hole in his chest and made a weird sound as he breathed. At last, one day, he died. It made me quite indignant to see all the rest, quite unconcerned, absorbed in their talk and games. Without thinking, I shouted, 'Stand up, everybody, and bow!' There was immediate silence, and all of them in the room leapt to their feet. Someone, apparently a non-commissioned officer, gave the order, and everyone bowed."[3]

II

As I have already said, human pain is at its greatest when a parent sends his child into suffering and lets him die. Because of the intensity of this pain, the "father and son" relationship is discussed in the pain of God. And, as we have noted, nothing is so self-centered and so particularistic as love between parent and child. This love is very *unequal*; nothing is so fatally destructive of ethics as inequality. Therefore, for all its intensity, love between parent and child *by itself* destroys a true ethic, and cannot be at all constructive. When the relation between parent and child was discussed in connection with the pain of God, only its intensity was considered, not the sinfulness which accompanies the human relationship between father and son. Therefore the pain of God is the primary word of the gospel; "the generation of the Son to the Father" must be secondary and subsidiary.

> The parent-child relationship is inevitably tainted by sinfulness. Not only: "all men who are born according to the course of nature are born in sin"[4]; love, which establishes the relation between parent and child, is already sinful. When the concept of the father-son relationship, which is centered in "generation," is applied to God, it becomes very imprecise. Furthermore, a father-son relationship free from sinfulness cannot be humanly understood. But with God the father-son relationship is free from sin. Therefore when the father-son relationship is applied to God, this concept is not precise, for the precise concept for the father-son relationship includes sinfulness. Augustine's confessions are again relevant here. We speak of the relation between father and son "not because this expression is appropriate, but because we cannot remain silent about it."[5]

The intensity of pain in the father-son relationship must be *sanctified* by the grace of the very pain of God. When Jesus commanded us to *hate* parents, wives, children, brothers, and sisters, he had this sanctification in mind. Our pain establishes the *ethic* by this sanctification. Its mark is the *equality* of the intensity of that pain. The ethic of pain is established when *all* the suffering neighbors share the pain a parent experiences by sending his son into suffering and letting him die. This is made possible by our being united into one body in the pain of God which embraces both our neighbors and us. "My love be with you all in Christ Jesus" (1 Cor. 16:24). But if this transcendent grace is not sought, the equality of love becomes unsound. This is the reason why Mo Ti's "universal love" is criticized as corrupting human ethics.

An ethic cannot have power unless it is tested by *experience*. Of course since *rinri* (ethics) is unalterably *ri* (reason), it must be a universal reason transcending individual experiences.[6] Mere "emotion" is not ethics. The more intense "emotion" is, the more unequal it is, and thereby equalization is made impossible. When "emotion" becomes "reason," an ethic with an equalizing principle can be established for the first time.

Nevertheless we cannot reach "reason" at a single leap. To reach the ethic of egalitarian "reason," must we not, using the medium of emotion (even though it is inegalitarian) to function as our springboard, then allow emotion itself to provide experience? Equalization of the intensity of pain is such a difficult problem that we are apt to regard the concept itself as inconsistent. In general, it would appear that, if the pain is intense, it could not be equal; and if it is equal, it would lose its intensity. But an ethic cannot be established in this way; invariably an ethic must aim at the equalization of intensity. Nevertheless, for the establishment of this ethic in the sense of glimpsing its possibility, the experience of "emotion" is demanded. It could be called experience as the premise of "reason"—primary experience, *Urerlebnis*, so to speak.

When we feel a love toward a suffering neighbor as intense as the love of a parent for his child—when we feel the same intensity of suffering toward a neighbor as that of a parent who sends his child into suffering—that experience will enable us to glimpse the possibility of the ethic of pain. There is no experience so blessed as this. It enables us to find *joy* even in the midst of suffering. It can be said that the ethic of pain is accompanied by joy. Previously we quoted Luther as saying that love proves itself not so much in sweetness and delight, but in very great sorrow and bitterness. In the middle of that passage, he says: "Because love is seemingly something soft and sweet, it is compared with the bit-

terest things," and, "according to Blessed Hilary, Christ was filled
with greatest joy by suffering the greatest pain. God 'is wonderful
in his saints.' Those who suffer the greatest pain rejoice most."[7]

III

We need not say that the commandment "You shall love your
neighbor as yourself" is the golden rule of the Christian ethic, and
that everything derives from it and returns to it. But I wonder if
one very important point has not been overlooked in the study of
this commandment. It is by no means limited to an ethical problem; it is of such a nature as deeply to influence theology itself.
The source of the problem lies in the fact that the "neighbors" in
this commandment include not only believers but, in most cases,
unbelievers. "Neighbor" is a concept applicable to anyone at
hand. The concept of neighbor is not valid if any sort of value
judgment is made on personality. "Neighbors" include unbelievers
as well as believers.

A most important conclusion must be deduced from this. If we
must love both believers and unbelievers as sincerely as we love
ourselves, and if this is what *God* commands us to do, we must see
unbelievers standing in the same "order of light" as believers. This
means that unbelievers should not perish any more than believers.
Usually we think that unbelievers, unlike believers, stand in the
"order of darkness," and we imagine that God does not love them
as tenderly as he loves believers; but this position cannot be sustained. An ethic which requires us to love unbelievers in the same
way that we love believers must develop into a *theology* that
places unbelievers and believers in the same "order of light." An
ethic which is the science of conduct utters a decisive word to a
theology which is the science of grace. One of the most difficult
problems of theology, namely, the problem concerning unbelievers, which, it has been supposed, could only be solved by the
banal idea of universal salvation, is now brightly illuminated by
ethics. To use a Kantian expression, a problem impossible to solve
in the dimension of theory can be solved in the dimension of
practice.

However, we must advance still further in our thinking. Ethics,

which is human love, has the love of God as its source. ". . .
love one another as I have loved you" (John 15:12). What sort
of love, then, is the love of God which forms the basis of love
toward unbelieving neighbors? Needless to say, it is the love of the
cross, that is, the pain of God. The love of God which accepts
unbelievers in this way is simply the pain of God, because it
accepts those who absolutely should not be accepted. Once again
we have demonstrated how ethics is established only by virtue of
the pain of God.

When the believer who has felt the pain of God in his heart
loves his unbelieving neighbor as intensely as himself, the unbeliever is borne on the body of the believer into God's pain. The
unbeliever stands in the immediate love of God—the reality of the
wrath of God. Yet through the love of the believer the unbeliever
is transferred from darkness into light. That is why the believer is
called "the light of the world" (Matt. 5:14). Light cannot limit its
brightness to itself; it inevitably shines on its dark surroundings
and illuminates them. "In making itself beautiful, the rose adorns
the garden." So it is with the *church* in the world of actuality.
Actuality in itself is doubtless darkness. But the church which is
immanent within that actuality tranforms it into light by its own
light. Nevertheless that light forever stems from the *transcendence*
of the church.

IV

At this point we must return again to the fundamental principle
of the gospel. When we use the term "pain of God" as the fundamental principle of the gospel, it points to two different aspects:
first, that the pain of God reflects his heart, loving those who
should not be loved; second, that the pain of God reflects his
heart, allowing his only Son to die. The first has its origin in the
second. In considering the "ethic of God's pain," our attention so
far has been directed to the second aspect. That is, we have tried
to recover in our ethic the very pain which God experienced when
he let his only Son die.

Now we must turn our attention to the first aspect. Our ethic
derives its power from the pain of God, from following God who

loves those who should not be loved. Sin is the betrayal of love. "Surely, as a faithless wife leaves her husband, so have you been faithless to me, O house of Israel, says the LORD" (Jer. 3:20). Sinners who never should be loved are betrayers of this love. Sin therefore presupposes intense love. When intense love is betrayed, anger becomes intense. Mediated by sin, the immediate love of God becomes the wrath of God. Yet the pain of God is the tidings that God *still* loves the sinner who has lost all claim to be loved. This is the love for "enemies" (Rom. 5:10). The mark that distinguishes the gospel from the law is to be sought solely in the pain of God. The law, in brief, is the will of God to love only those who are lovable. Therefore, the viewpoint which interprets love in the gospel as being only for objects worthy of love would reverse the whole gospel back to the law. This viewpoint is called "a different gospel" (Gal. 1:6).

In this sense there are many types of "different gospels." First, there is the classic type in Roman Catholicism, where God "forgives penitents because they are already sanctified within."[8] This means loving the sinner only after he has been changed into someone who is lovable. The Bible says, however: "But God shows his love for us in that while we were yet sinners Christ died for us" (Rom. 5:8).

A similar viewpoint can be seen in certain Protestant biblical interpretations. In fact, Protestants advocate this viewpoint more boldly than Catholics. Most commentators interpret the words "For I came not to call the righteous, but sinners" (Matt. 9:13= Mark 2:17=Luke 5:32) as follows: This is sarcasm directed against the Pharisees; "the righteous" is a term used to denote those who are actually worse than "the sinners," that is, hypocrites. But "sinners," because they already know themselves to be sinners, are essentially much better than the "righteous" and are therefore worthy of God's love. This is the reason why Jesus did not call "the righteous" but "sinners."[9]

There is still another school of thought which requires our careful attention. A distinction has been drawn between "sinners" and "the wicked." Sinners are subjectively wicked while the wicked are objectively sinners; sinners are those who, recognizing their sinfulness, repent and are forgiven by God. The wicked, on the other hand, become the enemies of God and Christ by their evil works. Therefore sinners are to be "respected," while the wicked are "unpardonable." Also, "that Christ is a friend of sinners does not mean that he is a friend of the wicked. Christ is not a friend of the wicked; when a man does evil he becomes the enemy of Christ."[10] Therefore "sinners" are not in fact the enemies of God, but only "those whom people in this false world call sinners." Christ is the friend of *these sinners*.[11] Those whom God loves are "sinners who have repented," "hearts which sorrow for their sins."[12] In short, these are *lovable sinners*.

It is certain that what we have here is completely different from the gospel of Paul and Luther. According to Paul, Christ died for us *while we were still enemies* (Rom. 5:10). Sinners are not lovable, but *hateful people*, "hated . . . and hating" (Titus 3:3). According to Luther, God did not save "false sinners," but "real sinners."[13] And for that reason, grace is not "false grace," but "real grace," *vera gratis*. It is this "real grace" which is the pain of God. All kinds of "different gospels" are alike in their denial of God's pain as the true grace.

Nygren's merit was that he clarified the character of the gospel by designating "false grace" as *eros* and "true grace" as *agape*. Though it may be said safely that in the last few decades few thinkers in theological circles have made such a substantial contribution as Nygren, we do not find him completely satisfactory. I would like to say a word about his thought here. According to Nygren, Christian love is seen most clearly in that God loves sinners. However, it is not because sinners are better in themselves than the righteous that God calls them and not the righteous. God's love in no way depends on the man who receives it; it is based completely on God himself. "Thus the question how far those whom God loves deserve his love falls to the ground."[14]

Up to this point we find ourselves in complete agreement with Nygren. But the problem arises when he says: "To the question, Why does God love? there is only one right answer: *Because it is his nature to love*."[15] This statement by itself may not be wrong, but it seems to have lost sight of something decisive—the pain of God. The concept of *agape* in Nygren, in spite of its clarity, is void of the pain of God. The love of God in the cross of Christ is superior to the love of God as his nature. Though Nygren speaks about the cross of Christ as being inseparable from *agape*, what he actually says is this: "*When Paul speaks of the cross of Christ, he is speaking of God's love and nothing else*."[16] With Nygren one cannot see the *cruciality* of the cross in *agape*. What difference is there between the words we have quoted and the following words of a liberal: "To Christian faith it belongs to the *nature* of God to impart himself in self-sacrificing love"[17]?

Let us further compare the words of these two theologians. Nygren: "If we had not seen love that is revealed in the Cross of Christ, we should not have known what love, in the Christian sense of the word, is. We should doubtless have known what love in general is, but not what love in its highest and deepest sense is."[18] Brown: "Thus it is not in any new teaching that we are to seek the distinctive Christian contribution to the thought of God, but in a living illustration of what the old teaching really meant."[19] In other words, Nygren does not take a clear-cut, decisive attitude toward the liberalism which rejects the pain of God.

For those of us who follow the Lord of the cross by bearing our cross and follow the pain of God by suffering pain, ethics must also be determined by the love of the cross—the pain of God. We must not limit ourselves to loving only those who are lovable (Luke 6:32-34). We must love the unlovable, and obey the commandment "Love your enemies, do good to those who hate you, bless those who curse you, pray for those who abuse you" (Luke 6:27-28, 35). We must be merciful as our Heavenly Father is merciful (vs. 36). This "mercy" requires *pain* itself. Just as the mark of the gospel is pain, so the mark of the Christian ethic is pain. When the gospel lacks the pain of God, it changes into a "different gospel" which loves only the lovable. Similarly, when ethics loses pain, it becomes the "love of sinners" which loves only the lovable (Luke 6:32-34). That the mark of the gospel is the pain of God means for us that God's love is an *immutable* love, "faithfulness" (Hos. 2:20). Following this, the fundamental character of the "ethic of pain" must be *constancy*. When our fellow becomes an "enemy" who betrays our love, and we continue to love him still more deeply, then pain is born in us. In an ethic without pain we love our fellow only as long as he is worthy of our love; then, when he is no longer worthy, we drop him and forget him. There is no constancy in such a love.

v

The true nature of the pain of God is to be found when it develops directly into a *love* that is rooted in his pain. If this is so, the true nature of the ethic of pain must be an ethic of love rooted in pain. We have already discussed what is meant by the pain of God developing into love rooted in his pain. The pain of God is destined to become real love which even forgets what it has forgiven. This is intent love rooted in the pain of God.

In this connection, we would like to draw attention to the doctrine of the church which is found in Ephesians 5:22-33. Here the relation of Christ and the church is likened to the relation of man and wife. First, Christ as the husband "gave himself up" for his wife, the church (vss. 25, 26)—"which he obtained with his own blood" (Acts 20:28). At this point particular stress is laid on the pain of God; in Ephesians 5:28-29 a totally new development is emphasized: "Even so husbands should love their wives as their own bodies. He who loves his wife loves himself. For no man ever hates his own flesh, but nourishes and cherishes it, as Christ does the church . . ." The relationship here mentioned no longer suggests love as the pain of God, such as seen in Hosea, but as corresponding to intense, immediate love. Here the intensity of the pain of God results in a return to immediacy. Love of one's fellow because one loves oneself is love in its immediacy. If the forgiveness of sin is real, the love which prompts it acquires the nature of immediate love. Love of the unlovable, when we are absolutely consistent in it, displays the power to transform the unlovable into the *lovable*. This is *sanctification*.

> Evangelical understanding contains the power of sanctification in forgiveness and sanctifies because of the forgiveness. On the other hand, as we have seen already, Catholicism takes the contrary view that forgiveness results from sanctification. The significance of the Reformation can be understood only by those who are acute enough to perceive this subtle difference.
>
> Here the relation between "sinners" and the "righteous" discussed above can find a new dimension. By the power of love rooted in God's pain, even real sinners may be changed into lovable people, people who are actually good. The "righteous," on the contrary, since they know only God's immediate love, and do not bathe in the love of God, may end up as "hypocrites" and actually bad people. However, this should be spoken of only in terms of sanctification as love rooted in the pain of God, not reconciliation as God's pain. The viewpoint of the "different gospels" which we criticized above confuses these two orders.

In this connection another limitation of Nygren's theology emerges clearly. Since the gospel, according to Nygren, is restricted to love for the unlovable, it excludes love for the lovable as *eros*. Therefore he cannot find a place for the reality of the love of God which is illustrated in Ephesians 5:22-33, cited above. That is, it is impossible for Nygren to speak of *love* rooted in God's pain. For that reason, Nygren does not speak of man's love toward God.

In the ethics of love based on pain, we must behave as though ours were an immediate love. That *intensity* which characterizes love for the lovable must be enacted at this stage; rather we must strive to enact it. But we can see a contradiction here. Immediate love is intense without effort. If there is effort, immediate love loses its characteristics. But as long as love rooted in pain is *ethics*, it must presuppose effort. Immediate love is prior to ethics; it is not "should" (*sollen*), but simply "to will" (*wollen*). And now we must try to restore this will (which is naturalistic!) to its proper status. But the willingness acquired by effort will no longer enable us to retain its natural intensity.

This is the reason why our ethics is bound to be frail. It is because of this that ethics must always remain unfulfilled. Because of the break in this ethic, we must return again and again to God's pain which is the forgiveness of sin. This is convincing evidence that love ought to be *rooted* in the pain of God.

VI

As Luther is our leader in matters of faith, so he is our leader in matters of *ethics*. To borrow Karl Holl's term, "the restructuring of morality" (*Der Neubau der Sittlichkeit*) was achieved by Luther. At this point a few words about him are necessary.

First of all, the "ethic of pain" was clearly conceived by Luther. Erich Seeberg states: "We conclude that Luther's ethics is determined by the law of *opposites*. To act well means to act *against one's own wishes*. God causes Christ and all his saints to do with their whole will what they least want to do. What one does not want to do he will do with all his might: this is the will and work of God. Thus Christ suffered in weakness, but willingly. This laying aside of his own will in ardent submission to the will of God makes it possible for him to acknowledge even as sweet and holy what in itself appeared so terrible and fatal."[20] To use Luther's own words, "Christ accomplished by a most fervent willingness what he did not wish (*noluntatem suam . . . ferventissima voluntate perfecit*). Thus God makes all his saints very willingly do what they do not want to do at all."[21]

If we act as we wish, we end by loving only the lovable, and thus we act wrongly. Since only loving the unlovable is "acting well," we must act contrary to our will. We must rather determine to do most fervently what is repugnant to us.

Concerning this point Luther dissociates himself from the ethical ideas of Augustine. In his excellent study *Augustins innere Entwicklung* (*Augustine's Inner Development*), Karl Holl shows that Augustine's ethic is controlled by the *idea of happiness*, and that he affirms *self-love* as the origin of ethics. "He always inserts the love of self between the love of God and the love of neighbor."[22] "The love of neighbor is to be evaluated according to the measure of the love of self."[23] This is why Holl refers to Augustine as one who "corrupted the Christian ethic."[24]

This immediately brings to mind the ethical thought of Kant. What Luther called the ethic of "not-willing" (*noluntas*) was inherited unchanged by Kant, who expressed it as "resistance" (*Widerstand*) against "inclinations" (*Neigung*). To follow one's "inclinations" is to behave unethically; to "resist" them is to behave ethically. This is what is usually called rigorism. It is not without reason that Kant has been called a "Protestant philosopher." The "ethic of pain" was given a precise scientific expression by Kant.

But Luther went a step further than Kant. With Luther the "ethic of pain" develops toward the "ethic of love rooted in pain," whereas Kant never reached this stage. According to Luther, true goodness is accompanied temporarily by "resistance," but it must break through this and arrive at the place where one can act "with free and joyous thoughts." As long as there is resistance, it is not truly good conduct. "Not-willingness" must become "willingness."

Here we must once more return to the thought of Augustine,

and find a place for it. Certainly love of neighbor must first pass through the negation of self-love, but if it is to be real love, it must result in the same genuine love that exists in self-love. Thus we see in Luther a synthesis of Augustine's ethic of willingness and Kant's ethic of not-willingness. Without this synthesis, it is impossible to make Augustine and Kant relevant. The straight line: Augustine–Kant–Luther, shows the development of ethics passing from *willingness* to *obligation*, then returning to *willingness* again. It is hardly necessary to point out that the willingness of the third stage differs in meaning from that of the first stage.

The development outlined above is consummately described by Holl: "For Luther, the relationship to an absolute demand does not exhaust the concept of the ethical. Rather for him a second and equally important characteristic enters in, namely, freedom; or, more precisely, the 'joy of willing' (*Freudigkeit des Wollens*). By joining these two together, Luther established a concept of the ethical which has never been expressed with this acuteness before or since. Kant merely advocated the nonrestrictive law—it is understandable that the romanticists criticized its one-sidedness— Augustine, on the other hand, demanded 'willingness' (*Willigkeit*), but he insisted on this in the mixture of ethical efforts with the idea of happiness. Luther surpassed them both [Augustine and Kant] by uniting what both of them had only half-discovered. He thought that the ethical could only be realized when duty (*Gesolltes*) becomes joyous will (*Gewolltes*), that is, when the 'law' is not only 'affirmed' but is accepted with warm feeling as appropriate to the situation of man."[25]

> In spite of this lucid exposition, certain questions about Holl's understanding of Luther remain. They are concerned with the *incompleteness* of ethics, which I discussed earlier. Only because an ethic is incomplete can Luther's "faith alone" be relevant. But Holl does not take this aspect seriously enough, and there is a strong tendency in him to emphasize Luther's ethical thought by itself. This is why Holl's standpoint can be criticized as being too Kantian and too moralistic.

Chapter Eight

The Immanence and Transcendence of the Pain of God

I

Matthew 25:31-46 comprises the last sermon which Jesus delivered on earth. I would like to study the truth contained in our Lord's words here in connection with the verses which follow in 26:6-13. I believe that by linking these two passages we learn a significant truth for our discussion.

Matthew 25:31-46 comprises Jesus' last sermon according to Matthew, and Jesus must have intended to deliver here a final, decisive, and important truth of the gospel. What is described is the judgment of God which will finally determine our destinies. Jesus shows most concretely what the criterion of this judgment is. If we state this criterion in essence, *to love historical reality* is to love God. "Truly, I say to you, as you did it to one of the least of these my brethren, you did it to me" (vs. 40). The destiny of salvation or destruction is determined by whether or not this love was practiced.

What we learn from this Scripture passage is that God expects us to love him not as an immediate object, but rather through our neighbors. That is, God becomes *immanent* in historical reality. Moreover the reality denoted here is reality in pain. Hungry, thirsty, a stranger, naked, sick, in prison—these are the realities of pain. God becomes *immanent* in these realities of pain: he says, "for I was hungry." Accordingly, service for the pain of God cannot be accomplished by itself, but only through service for the pain of reality. One who seeks to serve only the pain of God and does not seek to serve the pain of reality ultimately finds himself thwarted. ". . . as you did it not to one of the least of these, you did it not to me" (vs. 45).

The relation between the two great commandments corresponds to the truth indicated above (Matt. 22:37-40). According to Mark, the question which was asked Jesus was "Which commandment is the *first* of all?" (Mark 12:28). It would be reasonable to give only one answer to the question about the "first" commandment. Jesus gives the commandment to love God, and then says, "a second is like it," to love one's neighbor (Matt. 22:39). One cannot help thinking that love of God and love of neighbor are two—yet one, at the same time. It may be said that love of God is the large target, love of neighbor, the small one. If we wish to hit two targets at the same time with one arrow, we must be particularly careful about how we set up the targets. To love God "with all your heart, and with all your soul, and with all your mind," and really to love your neighbor "as yourself" is, in effect, to shoot at two targets with one arrow. For just as loving God with all our heart demands a singleness of heart, so does loving our neighbor. We do not love God with half our heart and love our neighbor with the other half: we love God with all our heart and our neighbor with all our heart. This is what hitting two targets with one arrow means. If the two targets, God and our neighbor, were set up side by side, we could not do it. However, if God, the large target, and our neighbor, the small target, stand one in front of the other, with the same center, we can hit both targets with one arrow. To hit the target (our neighbor) in the center means hitting the other target (God) in the center at the same time.

This relationship corresponds exactly to the immanence of the pain of God in the pain of reality, as discussed above. Because God is immanent in our neighbor, love of neighbor becomes love of God. Similarly, because the pain of God is immanent in the pain of reality, service for the pain of reality can become service for the pain of God.

II

Immediately *after* speaking about the immanence of the pain of God, Jesus went to the house of Simon in Bethany. But what happened in Bethany and the words spoken there by Jesus strike

us with the force of the unexpected. Our surprise and perplexity
are all the greater because these words were spoken immediately
after the sermon found in the latter part of Matthew 25.

"Now when Jesus was at Bethany in the house of Simon the
leper, a woman came up to him with an alabaster jar of very
expensive ointment, and she poured it on his head, as he sat at
table. But when the disciples saw it, they were indignant, saying,
'Why this waste? For this ointment might have been sold for a
large sum, and given to the poor'" (Matt. 26:6-9).

If we read the passage up to this point, we cannot help feeling
that the indignation of the disciples is justified. These disciples
are simply applying the truth which had just been taught by Jesus:
that giving to the poor is the only way of loving the Lord. It was
therefore natural for the disciples to expect words of approval and
praise from Jesus. But the reply of Jesus was quite unexpected.

"'Why do you trouble the woman? For she has done a beautiful thing to me. For you always have the poor with you, but you
will not always have me'" (Matt. 26:10-11).

According to Jesus, the woman had done a beautiful thing,
while the disciples, in troubling her, had done an ugly thing. The
words of the disciples, which were unmistakably an application of
what Jesus had just taught them, are now denied by him. If we
may express his words more sharply: "It's all right for the moment
to leave the poor as they are. Now I want you to think about me."
The significance of Jesus' words lies in the contrast between the
transcendence of Jesus and historical reality. Jesus transcends
reality infinitely. Before him, actuality pales into insignificance
and vanishes away. Jesus demands our wholehearted interest, and
for that reason will not allow us to be interested in actuality. Here
Jesus has the authority (*axioma*) which is derived from the principle (*axiom*). We must make up our minds to answer "Yes" to
his proclamation of the principle. "You will not always have me,"
are his words calling us to make the decision. The woman "did a
beautiful thing" because she dared to make the decision. But Jesus
continued: "'In pouring this ointment on my body she has done it
to prepare me for burial'" (vs. 12).

The true significance of this incident is revealed to us only with these words. When we understand their significance, we are shaken to the depths as if shocked by electricity. Listen! Jesus is about to be *buried*. God's only Son, God himself in the person of his Son, is about to be *buried!* We to whom this fact has been revealed forget *everything* else. We can no longer be interested in anything else. *God is in pain.* Before this fact all other actuality loses significance. Only those who are deeply concerned in God's pain to the point of even forgetting all other pains of actuality have truly seen the pain of God.

Jesus in Bethany reveals the *transcendence* of the pain of God. The pain of God which demands transcendence is the pain of God as *principle*. It is this transcendence that really characterizes the *gospel*. Those who serve the gospel must be like this woman. It is not surprising that Jesus bestowed the highest praise on her: " 'Truly, I say to you, wherever this gospel is preached in the whole world, what she has done will be told in memory of her' " (vs. 13).

III

We cannot say, however, that with the above considerations we have fathomed the whole truth about this matter.

We must take a further step in order to plumb the *heart of the gospel*. This step is taken when we *link* the Jesus of Bethany to the Jesus who spoke the words of Matthew 25. Final truth is to be found when we unite the immanence and the transcendence of the pain of God, that is, when the *axiom* contains present actuality within itself.

The gospel, that is, the pain of God, infinitely transcends the pain of the world, but why has it come into existence? What is the *object* of God's pain? It was born to save the *pains of the world* and to make the pains of the world its purpose. The Jesus of Bethany is the *same* Jesus who spoke the words of the 25th chapter of Matthew. The Lord who is completely immanent in the pain of the world can absolutely transcend it. *The pain of God, which transcends the pain of actuality, is still transcendent while immanent in it.* Even when the Lord asserts his transcendence, he does not cease to be immanent. Because the Lord teaches that giving to the poor is the only way to serve him, he can tell us momentarily to forget and neglect the poor. Because the *axiom* (principle) is realistic, it has the *axioma* (power) even to demand attention to itself to such an extent that reality may be forgotten.

Our assertion that the *axiom* holds the *axioma* should be compared with the *separation* (*chorismos*) in the Platonic sense. ". . . sells all that he has . . ." (Matt. 13:44, 46). To this extent we must be Platonists. According to Luther, evangelists can be called "solafideists" (*Solarii*).[1] We must also be "solafideists." In this respect Luther has something in common with the spirit of Plato. But Luther and those who follow him ought to know *more* than Plato.

Since the *axiom* is the pain of God, and the Kingdom of God is the reign of love based on God's *pain*, the *axioma* which belongs to the *axiom* is not simply "separation." It is an *axiom* which increases its own *axioma* by *loving* and *accompanying* (Emmanuel!) our historical reality. In the gospel "separation" is at the same time "accompaniment." Transcendent yet immanent, separate yet accompanied—this is the *heart of the gospel*. Its essence consists of solafideism which includes within itself an "and" with —at the same time—an "only." Here "and" is made captive by love within the "only."

IV

The pain of God, immanent as it is in man's reality, nevertheless transcends it. In the preceding pages we have considered this matter from God's side; now we must look at it from man's side.

It is doubtlessly true that the suffering of the "poor" (Matt. 26:9, 11) may be relieved temporarily by our charity. The immanence of God's pain has its significance here. But even though the poverty of the "poor" has been relieved and they are no longer poor men, the pain of these people has not thereby been completely resolved. Man's pain shows its true face on a deeper level than the pain which reveals itself in *actuality*: it is none other than *sin*. Poverty may be relieved by charity, but sin cannot. The solution for sin must be sought beyond charity, the act of immanent love. It must be found in God's pain which is his *forgiveness of sin*. When man tries to resolve his deepest suffering (beyond that which is on the surface), he, by surpassing immanent love, seeks transcendent love which forgives his sin. This is why Jesus proclaimed the forgiveness of sin to those who wished him to heal their sickness (Matt. 9:1-8).

When the pain of God loves the human condition, it first makes human pain its own, becomes one with it, becomes immanent in it, and then seeks to resolve the pain which is tangible. ". . . as you did it to one of the least of these my brethren, you did it to me" (Matt. 25:40). But since the true nature of human pain is to be found *beyond* the tangible suffering, the pain of God now transcends human pain and loves it in a way that embraces and supports its very roots. The true nature of man's condition lies in this: that it has nothing to support itself *within*. In a decisive crisis man becomes aware of this, and begins to seek his salvation in transcendent love.

It is possible, however, that some men may refuse to recognize their own condition. Indeed they may be of such a nature that they are not aware of it. But even in cases like this, the pain of God sees the actuality and loves it completely. "Loving it completely" means loving it as it actually is, not in terms of what it is not. Love must respect man's individuality. In this sense, the real nature of God's pain is expressed. Then Christians' *condolore* (suffering pain together) also becomes realistic. It is not without reason that Paul uses "anguish" (*odune*) for the first time in Romans 9:2.

Clearly the pain of God passes from immanence to transcendence because of his grace. The pain of God, since it is grace, becomes immanent first in human suffering, but, for this very reason, becomes transcendent. This is the act of grace. When grace becomes all-pervading, it shifts from immanence to transcendence. Because God's pain loves man's reality, it also discloses the real nature of man's pain through that which is visible. Even when God's pain has become transcendent, he has by no means abandoned his immanent love; on the contrary, he has *pervaded* it.

The *church* is the place where this pain of God is to be borne in this world. The pain of God actually takes place in the church, which is the body of Christ. The immanence and transcendence of the pain of God in their relation to human reality can be applied in exactly the same way in their relation to the church. How the church should love and serve the world can be assumed from what has been said in the preceding pages of this chapter.

Chapter Nine

The Pain of God
and the Hidden God

I

We should now like to consider a most important concept in the theology of Luther, the concept of the "hidden God" (*Deus absconditus*), and examine the connection which this concept has with the pain of God. Luther derived this concept from the Latin version of the words of Isaiah 45:15.[1] He brought a special meaning to these words and made them into a theological idiom. We cite a few typical passages:

"God hid his gracious will and his good purposes beneath his wrath and his punishment."[2] "God hid his eternal benevolence and mercy under his eternal wrath; he hid his righteousness under unrighteousness."[3] "For our good is hidden and that so deeply that it is hidden under its opposite. Thus our life is hidden under death, self-love under self-hatred, glory under shame, salvation under perdition, the kingdom under banishment, heaven under hell, wisdom under foolishness, righteousness under sin, strength under weakness. And generally, every yes we say to any good under a no, in order that our faith may be anchored in God, *who is the negative essence and goodness and wisdom and righteousness and whom we cannot possess or attain to except by the negation of all our affirmations.*"[4] "[God] has concealed his power only under weakness, his wisdom under foolishness, his goodness under austerity, his righteousness under sin, and his mercy under wrath. This is why many do not recognize God's power when they see his weakness, etc. It says in Psalm 81:7: 'I heard thee in the hiddenness of the tempest.' Notice that it says 'in the hiddenness,' which means: when the fury of his wrath hides the sweetness of his mercy, i.e., when he grants our prayers by doing the opposite of what we look for."[5] "For God's working must be hidden and we cannot understand its way. For it is concealed so that it appears to be contrary to what our minds can grasp."[6]

At first glance this concept of Luther's may appear to be derived from the German mystic Tauler, but there is a clear difference between the two. Erich Seeberg's view about this is appropriate. "With Luther, God is the hidden God because he works and creates life in the antitheses of suffering and death. With Tauler the religious idea that God creates in antithesis and in suffering, and therefore is hidden to reason and known only to faith, recedes. In the foreground is rather the philosophical notion of a God who is defined only through negation, and is therefore 'unknown' and 'hidden.' . . . The fundamental difference lies in its relationship to the revelatory concept. The hidden God is the God of revelation. The unknown God is the God who is enthroned beyond all revelation in the dark inaccessibility of his non-objective being."[7] (It is obvious from what is said here that the concept of the "hidden God" in our time, which frequently appears in Barth's early theology, differs from Luther's.)

The importance of Luther's "hidden God" has gradually been recognized, and has even finally come to be regarded as the most significant concept in his theology. According to Seeberg, this concept is "the fundamental principle of Luther's theology."[8] Kattenbusch says, "Only those who properly understand this 'hidden God' can thoroughly understand Luther."[9] It might be argued that these views have gone a little too far. I used to have some doubts about them, too. However, I have become convinced that this view is correct, and that in fact Luther's *whole theology* rests in the concept of the "hidden God." Let me summarize this position.

Apart from the idea of the "hidden God," two fundamental concepts emerge from Luther's theology: the first is the "righteousness of God," *iustitia Dei*; the second is "faith alone," *solo fide*. These two concepts stand in internal relation to each other. Objectively speaking, the gospel which Luther found is the "righteousness of God"; subjectively speaking, it is "faith alone."

As I see it, both of these concepts can be derived from that of the "hidden God," and can be considered as its *variations*. The righteousness of God revealed in the gospel stands in marked contrast to man's thought which strives to claim the righteousness of the law. It *destroys* this human righteousness, and yet is *hidden* under sin. Faith is the way which accepts this new righteousness of God *against* a man's own natural thinking and wisdom.

But the "hidden God" destroys human righteousness and reveals his own righteousness by confronting it. Could it be, then, that both the "righteousness of God" and "faith alone" are, after all, developed concepts of the "hidden God"? "Faith means believing in the hidden God, or recognizing the hidden God as God . . . Thus faith in the hidden God essentially coincides with faith in Christ."[10] "Faith therefore means accepting the hidden God, or, since the hidden God reveals himself distinctly in Christ, it also means affirming his incarnation in Christ."[11] In Luther's works the "hidden God" is most sharply described in *The Bondage of the Will* (*De servo arbitrio*). We may safely say that Luther valued this work more highly than any other of his writings because of the role this concept played in his thinking. For this reason I agree with the view that the concept of "hidden God" is the fundamental principle in Luther's theology, and that all the rest of his thoughts stem from it.

Not only does the "hidden God" determine Luther's theology; it also determines his *ethic*. For Luther, ethic emerges where love for God and neighbor is detached from self-love. How can freedom from self-love be realized? What does it mean to hate oneself? According to Luther, perfect self-negation and self-hatred is submitting "freely to the will of God whatever it may be, even for hell and eternal death, if God should will it, in order that his will may be fully done; it is seeking absolutely nothing for oneself."[12] But the God who sends man into hell and death in order to cleanse mankind is the "hidden God." Self-hatred can only be realized through the wrath of God which stands absolutely beyond man's self-controlling power. This is the reality of "hell and death" according to Luther. God sends man into hell and death, not to kill him, but to give him a real life. God hides his love beneath his wrath. Thus the "hidden God" creates self-hatred, destroys self-love, and thereby establishes a true ethic. Once again we may conclude that Luther's thought is determined by the concept of the "hidden God."

II

Luther's "hidden God" is important because the concept is fundamental to our faith; we cannot live a Christian life without it. In this thought resounds the triumphant song of faith echoing throughout the Bible. Luther's hymn "A Mighty Fortress Is Our God" shows the climax of his faith in the "hidden God."

The theological basis for the concept of the "hidden God" is this: the wrath of God is the *means* of revealing his love. Consequently faith is to have an insight into God's love veiled *under* his wrath. It is difficult to measure how much comfort, joy, and strength this thought brings to a Christian's life.

However, we cannot overlook one great *problem* in connection with this idea. That is, is it sufficient to consider the wrath of God only as the "means" of revealing his love? Rather is it not true that the wrath of God implies something other than the means of revealing his love? Paul Althaus, for instance, says that the theology which regards the wrath of God simply as a means for his love reduces it to a "unitary concept of God," and therefore cannot be adequate for the "theology of faith."[13]

In other words, before the wrath of God becomes the means for his love, it is the reality in conflict with his love. This is the biblical point of view as such. Luther's experience of the wrath of God was fearful enough to "turn his bones into ashes."[14] Moreover, the experience of his judgment under the wrath of God became the starting point for his inner development. It is most regrettable that this fundamental experience of his could not have been utilized fully in his central thought, the "hidden God."

The concept of the "hidden God" gives more difficulty when

Luther attempts to apply it to *Christ* as well as to the believers. Let me cite Luther's typical passage in this regard: "For God's working must be hidden, and we cannot understand its way. For it is concealed so that it appears to be contrary to what our minds can grasp . . . In this way he acted in his own proper work, in that which is the foremost of his works and the pattern of them, i.e., in Christ. When he wanted to glorify him and establish him in his Kingship, he made him die, he caused him to be confounded and to descend into hell."[15] Since Christ is the example (*exemplum*) as well as the gift (*donum*) to the believers, these words are not inapplicable, but the significance of Christ's death must be found elsewhere. The wrath of God which Christ bore in himself was never a means for his love, but rather his actual response to man's rebellion.

When the love of God bears and overcomes his wrath, nothing but the *pain of God* takes place. The solution of the wrath of God must be sought in the pain of God before it can be sought in the "hidden God." In Luther's thought some idea corresponding to that of the pain of God can be found.[16]

It is now possible to see the mutual relationship of the two concepts: the "hidden God" and the pain of God. Because Christ has already overcome the reality of God's wrath, we are allowed to perceive it in faith as a *means* for his love. Faith in the "hidden God" becomes a truth only after it finds its basis in the pain of God. Love rooted in the pain of God provides the place where faith in the "hidden God" can be realized. Because of God's love, the wrath of God can be used as a means.

Luther probably left the difficulty unresolved because he confused the dimension of love rooted in the pain of God—where the concept of the "hidden God" should be established—with the dimension of the pain of God. I believe that Luther seriously thought about the pain of God. But he was confused in the way he expressed the theological view of the "hidden God." The following criticism of Althaus is appropriate here: "A theology which conceives of the wrath of God as 'foreign work' in preparation for revealing his love, and therefore fundamentally as love, does not express fully the Christian experience of God which is living yet imperfect. Reflection (*Rückschau*) may gratefully see wrath and love as one, and consider God's love as the permeation of his holiness. But reflection itself is only one pole of our life. In living movement (and when will we transcend it?) we experience God's love as salvation from his judgment."[17] "But then I see his love which has laid hold of me not in the same direction with his wrath, but as a powerful counter-movement, as a breach in the barrier. From this we come to the doctrine of the cross, which describes God's forgiving love as having conquered his wrath."[18] For me this doctrine of the cross is really a description of the pain of God.

III

The following sentences, which I wrote in my student days, may be relevant to the topic under discussion. With the exception of a few terms, the line of thought is the same as what I hold at present, and I shall quote them as they stand.

The Pain of God and the "Hidden God"

In Romans 5:3 Paul uses the words "we rejoice in our sufferings." How could he use words like these? The God who afflicted Paul and made him suffer must have appeared as a God of wrath. Yet when Paul suffered, he was not crushed, but was able to "rejoice." This was because he saw a deeper meaning in his suffering—he saw through God's wrath and perceived his love beyond it. And the God who brings suffering on those he loves, the God who executes his wrath as a means for love, is the "hidden God" (*Deus absconditus*), according to Luther. Thus Paul demonstrates in this text that he was able to retain his faith in the "hidden God."

Next, in Romans 11:32, Paul says, ". . . God has consigned all men to disobedience, that he may have mercy upon all." To express it more sharply, it means that God dares even to cast us down into sin in order that he may have mercy on us. Luther says, "God now and then lets man fall into sin" (*darumb . . . got . . . auch zu weilen ynn sund fallen lassit*).[19] But how could Paul, bearing these sins as his own responsibility, regard a God who would do things like this as a "merciful God"? This he could do because, as in the case mentioned above, he could cling to his faith in the "hidden God." For the "hidden God" not only hid his love under his wrath, but also "hid righteousness under unrighteousness" (*abscondit . . . justitiam sub iniquitate*).[20]

However a most important question arises here: Where do we have the basis for believing the wrath of God as revealed to us is merely a means for his love? In other words, we need to clarify the sure formulation for faith in the "hidden God." Even when God displays his wrath in order to reveal his love, do we not sink in despair by taking it as his *real* wrath and thus considering it as a sign that we are really forsaken? Where do we find the assurance that we are the objects of God's love, even if we try to think of that wrath as the means of love? How can we rid ourselves of Satan's whisper that faith in the "hidden God" is no more than our self-complacency, attempting to protect the peace of our souls from being disturbed?

Paul gives the answer to this question in Romans 5:1, and the words of verse 1 are the premise of verse 3. In verse 1 he says: "Therefore, since we are justified by faith, we have peace with God through our Lord Jesus Christ." Here Paul is saying that though he was once the object of the *real* wrath of God, he is so no longer, and he has now obtained peace with God since Jesus Christ bore the real wrath for him and overcame it. Clearly Paul was able to consider God's wrath as merely a *means* for his love only because God revealed the fact that his *real* wrath has already been overcome by his love. When the love of God is trying to conquer and pierce through his wrath, this is called the *pain of God*.

Paul could hold fast to his belief in the "hidden God" because the "pain of God" was revealed to him in the cross of Christ. Thus, faith in the "hidden God" finds solid foundation in the "pain of God." Only those who are shown the wrath of God conquered by his love can believe the former is merely a *means* for the latter.

The love of God which loves only those who love, fear, and obey God may be called simply "God's love." But the love which loves sinners who become his "enemies" is called "God's love rooted in the *pain of God*." And the "pain of God" means this coexistence of the wrath of God with the love of God in tension.

This is how the *"love of God* rooted in pain" comes into being. The *love of God* sprung from his wrath comes into existence because his love conquers and pierces through the realm of his wrath. This is possible since the wrath of God is a "secondary work" (*opus alienum*), and the love of God is his "primary work" (*opus proprium*). And "love of God rooted in his pain" is his grace and mercy.

Let us compare the concept of the "hidden God" and that of the "pain of God." With the former, the wrath of God is considered as a *means* for his love, the "wrath of compassion" (*ira benignitatis*); whereas, with the latter, the wrath of God is real, the "wrath of severity" (*ira severitatis*). In the case of the "hidden God," he exercises love through his wrath; whereas, in the "pain of God," he exercises love by overcoming it. Therefore, as indicated above, the former can be sustained only when it is based on the latter.

Kattenbusch's phrase "the inner compatibility of the wrath of God and love" (*die innere Verträglichkeit von Zorn und Liebe*) can be appropriate for the "hidden God," but not for the "pain of God." For, with the "pain of God," wrath and love cannot be compatible; wrath must be overcome by love. The unity of wrath and love at the cross of Christ was not a unity without conflict, but it was a unity of victory gained after awful conflict.[21]

IV

The concept of the "hidden God" can be realized only in the sense of "love rooted in the pain of God." This relationship is seen clearly in the following passage from Luther: "They submit freely to the will of God whatever it may be, even for hell and eternal death, if God should will it, in order that his will may be fully done; they seek absolutely nothing for themselves. And yet, inasmuch as they themselves so purely conform to the will of God, they cannot possibly remain in hell. For one who surrenders his own self completely to the will of God cannot possibly be forever outside God. For he wills what God wills. Therefore he pleases God. And when he pleases God, he is loved by him and by this love he is saved. . . . But the true saints actually achieve this resignation, because their hearts overflow with love, and they do this without great distress . . . because of this very readiness, they escape from such a punishment. Indeed, they do not need to fear that they will be damned, because they submit gladly and willingly to damnation for God's sake."[22]

The "resignation to hell" (*resignatio ad infernum*), which is mentioned in the first stage of the above passage, implies self-hatred because we identify ourselves with suffering through God's pain and thus through his wrath. But when we put ourselves in pain, the light of God's love comes shining into the very midst of that pain. We are then delivered from pain by this love. It is certainly not accidental that we are delivered from the first stage of pain to the second stage of love. It follows necessarily from God's truth that his pain is the expression of love rooted in pain. The purpose of the above passage therefore is to describe not the psychology of faith, but emphatically the theology of grace.

Death is the most acute evidence of the wrath under which God may hide his love. In this way death is an indication not only of God's wrath, but also of his love. According to Paul, death as the "wages of sin" simply means darkness (Rom. 6:23). But Paul also says this death is the only possible way "to depart and be with Christ" (Phil. 1:23). Thus death is both to be avoided and to be desired. For those perishing, death is the process of accumulating God's wrath, and its end is annihilation. For those who are saved, death is the process of the consummation of God's love, and its end is sanctification and liberation from the mortal body. Furthermore, the resurrection of the dead body is evidence of this sanctification.

v

The concept of the "hidden God" implies his pain, and, conversely, his pain implies his "hiddenness." In support of the first idea, let us note the following passage from Luther: "We . . . cannot glorify God unless we do what we do not want to do . . . So then: 'to take up your cross' and 'to become Christ's disciple' (Luke 14:27) and 'to be transformed by the renewing of your mind,' etc., is the same as to hate yourself, to will against your own will, to mind what transcends your comprehension, to concede over against the objection of your own righteousness that you are sinful, and to give an ear to foolishness against the objection of your own wisdom."[23] We render service to the pain of God through our own pain by bearing our cross and following the Lord of the cross. We manifest our own pain by willing against our own will and hating ourselves. Luther is thus describing this truth in his concept of the "hidden God." We can reasonably conclude that the "hidden God" is the "pain of God."

The second concept is that "God's pain" is the "hidden God." This relationship is most clearly shown in Luther's phrase "God hidden in pain" (*Deus absconditus in passionibus*). Again, Luther says that the "crucified God" (*Deus crucifixis*) is at the same time the "hidden God"(*Deus absconditus*). We must now seriously consider this relationship.

The God "revealed" (*Deus revelatus*) to sinners can only be the God in pain, the God of the cross. And could God be any more *hidden* than when he was crucified and suffering on the cross? In this state he would appear to be someone other than God. Man, with his natural viewpoint, cannot see God in this state. The word of the cross is "a stumbling block to Jews and folly to Gentiles" (1 Cor. 1:23). In order to see the "revealed" God" in the "hidden God" we must receive the power of the *Holy Spirit* as a transcendent gift from God himself. " . . . no one can say 'Jesus is Lord' except by the Holy Spirit" (1 Cor. 12:3).

Philosophy in its seeking after God has continued to grasp for his image. Today philosophy has perhaps come closest to a true understanding of the image of God, and the very image of God in pain seems already to have been perceived. However, philosophy cannot recognize *Jesus of Nazareth* as the God in pain, for the leap to this confession can be accomplished only through the Holy Spirit. This wisdom is theology. God in pain is no more than the "hidden God" for the philosopher. Only the Holy Spirit can bring repentance. This repentance may be considered as a turning from man's search for God to God's search for man. If philosophy, which is basically the search for God, turns its direction (this is repentance), it becomes theology, witnessing to God the seeker after man.

God hid himself wholly when in the person of his only Son he passed through death, but this does not mean he lost his own existence. Even in the event of the cross there is no single change in the God who is the "I am that I am." How could this be possible? It is because God continues to live in the person of the Father while dying in the person of the Son. The death of God the Son can be called the pain of God because the person of the Father lived. Pain can only be experienced by the living, not by the dead who are already freed from suffering. Because God is essentially one in his essence, although Father and Son differ in the persons of the Trinity, it is possible that the Father still lives even in the death of his Son. Thus the pain of God arises. The death of God the Son was real death, and its darkness was real pain. God the Father who hid himself in the death of God the Son is God in pain. Therefore the pain of God is neither merely the pain of God the Son, nor merely the pain of God the Father, but the pain of the two persons who are essentially one.

> For this reason our term "pain of God" should be clearly distinguished from other synonyms. Not only must it be distinguished from the Sabellian heresy of Patripassianism, but also from what Ignatius calls the "suffering of our God" (*tou pathous tou theou mou,* on Rom. 6:3) and, more recently, Baillie's term the "suffering love of God."[24] The former position indicates only the sufferings of Jesus on earth, while the latter reflects a liberal viewpoint which sees God's love from the general principle of self-sacrifice on behalf of loved ones. Also the "pain of God" must be differentiated from such expressions often used in church prayers as "We cause thee to suffer by our sins." What we call the "pain of God" is not simply the response of his heart at our sins. It is the *wrath of God,* and not his pain, which responds to sin. Expressions such as "We cause thee to suffer by our sins" should be rejected as sentimental. God is angry at our sins, never hurt. God suffers pain only when he tries to *love* us, the objects of his wrath.

A father is never hidden so completely as when he sends his beloved son to suffer and, finally, to die. God is truly a "hidden God" in this sense. Abraham had to trample *ethics* underfoot when he was about to kill his son in order to serve God. (Kierkegaard has already pointed this out in *Fear and Trembling.*) When a father sacrifices his son in death, he must tear himself away from his fatherly nature. God the Father was the "hidden God" in the sense that he sacrificed his Son.

However, the "hidden God" implies at its deepest that he him-self has the pain in his essence. Christ considered death as his own essence. He is "the Lamb slain from the foundation of the world" (Rev. 13:8).[25] Christ's whole life was under a "sort of perpetual cross" (*perpetua crucis speciem*).[26]

Chapter Ten

The Order of Love

I

It may be advantageous at this point for us to summarize the progress of our previous discussion. To summarize is to set in order. Broadly speaking, the object of our thought has been the love of God. We shall now attempt in this chapter a systematization of the love of God. Following Augustine and Pascal, we shall call it the "order of love" (*ordo amoris*).

The concept "love rooted in the pain of God" expresses the whole of God's love. God's love can be divided into *three orders of love*. The first is the immediate "love of God"; the second is the "pain of God"; and the third is love rooted in the pain of God, which, for convenience, we shall call the "love . . . of God." When these three orders of love, by being united, comprise "love rooted in the pain of God," the truth really exists. Let us consider this truth by separating its orders.

1. THE LOVE OF GOD

This love of God pours *immediately* on its object without any hindrance. The object of this love is the person worthy of receiving it. This immediate "love of God" is expressed in the father-son relationship when God the Father loves his completely obedient Son. We must consider such a Son, who deserves his Father's love, as none other than God the Son, Jesus Christ. The love of God the Father toward God the Son, Jesus Christ, is the first order of

God's love revealed in Scripture (Matt. 3:17; John 3:35; 5:20; 10:17; 15:9-10; 17:23-26).

As long as men in general are worthy of God's love, they can be regarded as objects of this love. "When Israel was a child, I loved him, and out of Egypt I called my son. . . . I led them with cords of compassion, with the bands of love, and I became to them as one who eases the yoke on their jaws, and I bent down to them and fed them" (Hos. 11:1, 4). The Gospel of Matthew quotes the words "out of Egypt I called my son" as referring to Jesus, although they were originally spoken of the people of Israel. From this we may infer that both Jesus and mankind can be objects of God's love. Love of the first order was expressed in the parable of the Prodigal Son (Luke 15:11 ff.) when the father poured out his love on the younger son before he left for the far country.

This type of God's love may be characterized as smooth, flowing, and intense. In terms of human relationships, this may be called parental love. When we follow this divine love, we love our neighbors as our family, but it is love that exceeds even that of a blood relative. In the spiritual world, this love is the source of light and happiness; without it there would be darkness, and men would be infinitely miserable. Because of love the universe moves in its mighty path.

Both Christ and man were originally objects of God's love of the first order, but now only Christ is its object. Man has now *fallen* away from this kind of God's love, and has become unworthy of it because of rebellion and sin. Having become a prodigal son, he forfeited the love of his father. "The more I called them, the more they went from me . . ." (Hos. 11:2). The greatest betrayal of love is duplicity. "Their heart is false" (Hos. 10:2). Love betrayed can only turn to anger. When love is confronted with duplicity, it becomes angry and rejects its object. "Ephraim is joined to idols, let him alone" (Hos. 4:17). "Therefore God gave them up in the lusts of their hearts to impurity, to the dishonoring of their bodies among themselves . . . For this reason God gave them up to dishonorable passions" (Rom. 1:24, 26). The righteousness of God demands that unrighteousness be removed. It is improper for righteousness to be involved with unrighteousness. God is pure. Sinners "die in the shadow of God's wrath." Hell speaks of itself: "SACRED JUSTICE MOVED MY ARCHITECT./I WAS RAISED HERE BY DIVINE OMNIPOTENCE,/PRIMOR-DIAL LOVE AND ULTIMATE INTELLIGENCE."[1] God's indignation is nothing but the result of his "primordial love." This is the outcome of God's love of the first order, as far as we are concerned.

Were man permitted to imitate this type of God's love (though in fact he is himself the object of God's wrath), he would become angry with his fellowman, and, rejecting that person's unrighteousness and impurity, would say, "He is he; I am I." "Mercy and Justice deny them even a name./ Let us not speak of them: Look, and pass on."[2] A man incapable of anger should be despised. We would call such a man spineless. A man of integrity rightly rejects a man of deceit.

2. THE PAIN OF GOD

Because God acts in a way that seems "ungodlike," and "improper," the gospel is hard to believe. This is necessary for God to *forgive sins*. God did not repulse those who should be repulsed; he enfolded and *embraced* them. God appears to have become spineless! But this is the gospel to be believed and accepted: "How can I give you up, O Ephraim! How can I hand you over, O Israel! . . . My heart recoils within me, my compassion grows warm and tender" (Hos. 11:8). "I will heal their faithlessness; I will love them freely, for my anger has turned from them" (Hos. 14:4). Therefore we sinners can only say: "Come, let us return to the LORD; for he has torn, that he may heal us; he has stricken, and he will bind us up" (Hos. 6:1).

The gospel, however, appears to be folly (1 Cor. 1:18, 21, 23, 25). To the devout older son, the father who joyfully welcomed back his prodigal son must have seemed spineless (Luke 15:28 ff.). Thus God suffered pain in his forgiveness. "Is Ephraim my dear son? Is he my darling child? For as often as I speak against him, I do remember him still. Therefore my heart is troubled for him" (Jer. 31:20). This pain appeared in the shame of the cross which God accepted in the person of his Son.

Thus, those of us who would follow this second type of God's love must bear "abuse for him" (Heb. 13:13). We may appear to be spineless when we forgive and embrace those who should not be forgiven. This very shame constitutes our pain.

But for us human beings forgiveness does not create real pain. For those of us who forgive others are sinners before God and need his forgiveness just as those whom we forgive are. Only God really suffers pain in his forgiveness. With God sin should never be forgiven. "Sin is the death of God. Die sin must or God."[3] And yet this God forgives sin!

The pain of God, which results from his love of the second order, has a double meaning. First, it is God's pain in the sense that he forgives and loves those who should not be forgiven; secondly, it is his pain in the sense that he sends his only beloved Son to suffer, even unto death.

We have observed in our discussion on love of the first order that both Christ and we human beings are the objects of God's love, but that in reality Christ alone remains the object of his love. Now, in the second order of God's love, an astonishing thing has happened. Christ has separated himself from the love of God the Father and stepped into suffering and death to save lost mankind. Christ, the original object of God's love, dared to separate himself from this love for the sake of us lost ones, and endured the wrath of God in our stead. What an astonishing event! This is the pain of God—that he sent his only beloved Son to suffer and die for the salvation of us sinners. The suffering and death which Jesus had to endure reflect, in fact, the reality of the wrath of God. Here the double meaning of the pain of God is united into one.

We are jolted awake by the wonder of this grace; we bitterly repent our sins and begin to hate ourselves. Learning from the pain of God, we endeavor to serve him by experiencing a similar pain when we send our dear ones to suffer. As we have seen, however, our loved ones are the objects of our love according to the first order of love. They are the objects of the so-called "parental love." Thus the objects of our love of the first order become indispensable in realizing love of the second order.

3. "LOVE ... OF GOD"

God, who appeared to have ceased being divine, actually demonstrates his godliness when sinners become completely obedient to him by the pain of his forgiving love. The victory of his pain is in fact love rooted in the pain of God. This is why the Hebrew words translated "My heart is troubled," in Jeremiah 31:20, can also be rendered as "yearning" and "compassion" in Isaiah 63:15. By his love God once again becomes our Father. "For thou art our Father, though Abraham does not know us and Israel does not acknowledge us; thou, O LORD, art our Father" (Isa. 63:16). He is not a father in the immediate sense, but Father as "Redeemer" (same verse), mediated by and rooted in the pain of God. He made us his sons with Christ. There are, however, distinct differences between Christ's natural Sonship and our sonship through his redemption. This is the reason why Christ is called the "first-born" (Rom. 8:29).

The "love . . . of God" as the victory of his pain points to Christ's *resurrection* from the dead. Christ vanquished all things and became Lord of all by saving sinners and overcoming sin and death which encompassed them. God liberated Christ from death. On the third day the Lord rose, ascended into heaven, and sat at the right hand of God the Father. Then for the first time was God's pain healed. God the Father, who had sent his only beloved Son far away, made him suffer and die, now received him close to his side. How great the joy of the Father must be!

When we are allowed to follow this love of God, we shall also be permitted to pray that we may welcome back again to our side the dear ones whom we have sent out to suffer. Because of the "love . . . of God," we are permitted to pray that they may be saved from suffering. How can the love which does not percolate with power be the *love of God?*

The "ethic of pain" must become an "ethic of love" because it is an *ethic*. While the "ethic of pain" means that we "weep with those who weep," the "ethic of love" means that we "rejoice with those who rejoice."

The characteristics of the third order of love are to be seen in the recovery of the smooth, flowing, intense nature of the first order of love. "But while he was yet at a distance, his father saw him and had compassion, and ran and embraced him and kissed him" (Luke 15:20). This is intense love.

We who follow this love of God must also make the ethic based on forgiveness as alive as the ethic of intent love is. The ethic born of the "love . . . of God" can also be thought of as an ethic rooted in faith. The ethic that exists between one believer and another must follow the "love . . . of God" and must develop its smooth, flowing, and intense quality.

Living examples of this ethic can be found in the tender love displayed by Paul toward Timothy and Titus. Paul calls Timothy "my true child in the faith" (1 Tim. 1:2), "my beloved child" (2 Tim. 1:2), and Titus "my true child in a common faith" (Titus 1:4). ". . . I remember you constantly in my prayers. As I remember your tears, I long night and day to see you, that I may be filled with joy" (2 Tim. 1:3-4).

The intensity of love and pain expressed in these words move the readers to tears. And yet, this love is not simply immediate, human tenderness, but tenderness based on faith, which finds such an expression as the following words "I am reminded of your sincere faith" (2 Tim. 1:5). (In spite of the view that Paul is not the author of the Pastoral Letters, I would like to think that at least these passages which show Paul's love for Timothy and Titus reflect Paul's personality.)

A believer, particularly a minister, should be ashamed of himself as unworthy if he does not have an experience of this love. For a minister, this experience is primary and everything else secondary. If he has such an experience, nobody in the world is as blessed as he. By experiencing this "emotion," the "logic" of ethics finds a way to be realistic. ". . . we were gentle among you, like a nurse taking care of her children. So, being affectionately desirous of you, we were ready to share with you not only the gospel of God but also our own selves . . ." (1 Thess. 2:7-8).

One decisive matter still needs to be discussed in our study on the "order of love." That is, the *three* orders of love are seen inclusively in the one order—the "pain of God."

First, God's immediate love is not applicable to us, for in our sinful condition it becomes his wrath. This "wrath" of God can only exist by being upheld and included in his "pain,"which overcomes his wrath. Secondly, the "love . . . of God" is constantly being shipwrecked, although it is able to exist in our midst. This statement is expressed in the words of Isaiah 63:15: "The yearning of thy heart and thy compassion are withheld from me." Although our sins are dead, they are still rebellious enough to cause the shipwreck of the "love . . . of God." In spite of this shipwreck of his love, God still maintains his righteousness, being always in pain. God can be eternally righteous only when the "love . . . of God" stands inclusively in his "pain." Therefore with God the pain must be all-inclusive and eternal. ". . . our Redeemer from of old is thy name" (Isa. 63:16). "For I decided to know nothing among you except Jesus Christ and him crucified" (1 Cor. 2:2). Only the cross, only grace, only faith: ministers must be solafideists with Luther.

For us, the imitators of God's love, ethics must also mean, in the final analysis, that forgiveness is everything. Even though our love, along with God's love, is defeated and has become a "lost love," *verlorene Liebe*,[4] as Luther calls it, we must love our fellowmen with unchanging faithfulness as God has done (Hos. 2:20). Only then can our ethics acquire constancy. Love cannot help becoming *hope*. In ethics, patience which springs from hope is indispensable (Rom. 8:24-25).

II

In this section I would like to consider the order of love from a slightly different angle. The Lord's wounds heal our wounds, and God's pain saves our pain. The cross of the Lord is a sheltering rock from the tempest, a hiding-place in the desert. When we are within the pain of God, we are *protected*. How does this happen?

What actually smites and destroys us is the *wrath* of God. But the "pain of God" results from the love of the one who intercepts and blocks his wrath toward us, the one who himself is smitten by his wrath. Because God's pain has intercepted his wrath, those within his pain are protected. Thus pain, which is love of the second order, resolves the wrath into which love of the first order has turned. Here God's pain can possess the actual power to protect us.

However, our protection means that we have already been transported into God's intent love. In other words, we are speaking of the love of the third order. "My soul is feasted as with marrow and fat, and my mouth praises thee with joyful lips, when I think of thee upon my bed, and meditate on thee in the watches of the night; for thou hast been my help, and in the shadow of thy wings I sing for joy. My soul clings to thee; thy right hand upholds me" (Ps. 63:5-8). "Even though I walk through the valley of the shadow of death, I fear no evil; for thou art with me . . ." (Ps. 23:4).

Thus the meaning of God's three orders of love has become clear to us. What we must particularly observe here is that it is the second order itself which brings us from the first to the third order. The first and the third orders are both contained in the second. Accordingly both the first and the third are derived from the second order. That is why the second order of love is called a theological axiom.

When we are within the pain of God we are protected. God's pain is truly our peaceful abode. "Thy wounds will become/My dwelling-place on earth."[5]

Luke 12:4-7 (Matt. 10:28-31) speaks most clearly and powerfully of the relation of the orders of love which we have been discussing.

> "I tell you, my friends, do not fear those who kill the body, and after that have no more that they can do. But I will warn you whom to fear: fear him who, after he has killed, has power to cast into hell; yes, I tell you, fear him!" (vss. 4-5).
> "Are not five sparrows sold for two pennies? And not one of them is forgotten before God. Why, even the hairs of your head are all numbered. Fear not; you are of more value than many sparrows" (vss. 6-7).

To careful readers it will become clear that the first half of this passage, verses 4 and 5, stands in marked contrast to the second half, verses 6 and 7. Jesus spoke these two contrasting logia in deliberate succession, one after the other. This, I believe, can be assumed from the fact that both Matthew and Luke, in spite of a striking difference of context in the verses that precede and follow, record them together in the order which we find. In what sense, then, are these two logia contrasted to each other?

In the former we are warned about him who is to be feared; in the latter we are told of him who is to be trusted wholeheartedly without fear. The contrast lies between the verb "fear" of verse 5, and "fear not" of verse 7. In short, the former indicates the object of fear, while the latter indicates the object of trust.

The general meaning of the above verses should now be clear, but the deepest mystery of God's words needs further explanation. The first half of the two logia indicates the object of fear, and the second, the object of trust. If these objects were quite different in nature, this contrast might be insignificant and would not have either a deep truth or a mystery within itself. The conventional exposition is that the object of fear is something like Satan, while the object of trust is God. (A little thought will show that the Satan referred to is not the one to be feared of verse 5, but the one not to be feared of verse 4.)

I believe that we must regard both the object of fear in the first half of the saying and the object of trust in the second half as one and the same God. (As a matter of fact, most commentators interpret verse 5 as referring to God.) The same God is the object of fear on the one hand, and the object of complete trust on the other. Thus the form of this Scripture becomes clear.

But we must go one step further. It can be said, of course, that the same God is the object of both fear and trust: God who is feared is known to the evildoers; God who is trusted is known to the good. However, this type of interpretation is too superficial and lacks insight and depth. As a matter of fact, the text itself excludes such an interpretation. For the "you" who are addressed as the subject of the verb "fear" in verse 5 are the same "you" who are addressed in verse 7: These are the same people who are bidden both to fear and to trust. God of fear and trust does not separate the objects in two different categories, but rather approaches one and the same object with these double requirements. Thus we have reached the truth of the mystery which is contained in this Scripture. We must explore this mystery now.

Though any power outside of God is capable of destroying us, it cannot destroy us completely. But *God* can. For this very reason, we must not fear anything but God, and him only. God, unrelenting until he has completely destroyed us—this is the God of wrath. This God is reigning over us. So Jesus says, ". . . yes, I tell you, fear him!"

But immediately after this ". . . yes, I tell you, fear him!" Jesus abruptly says, "Are not five sparrows . . ." What are we told here? Nothing less than this: that God loves and protects us to the point that "even the hairs of your head are all numbered." That is why Jesus says, "Fear not." God's intent love for us, our intent trust in his love—this is the theme of the passage.

But is it not too abrupt a transition for the subject of the second half of the saying, which is the love of God, to be joined to the first half, which is the wrath of God? Certainly, it is abrupt. But we should never conclude that these are two unconnected sayings which were uttered on different occasions, and later accidently joined together. We must explore the meaning of this abruptness. The secret of the gospel truth lies within it.

The very Jesus who spoke these words is the heart of the secret. Jesus stands at the turning point from the theme of the first part to that of the second part. Let me illustrate this truth by a parable.

A traveler is walking across a field in summer, when suddenly a thunderstorm breaks out above him. There is neither tree nor habitation; the traveler must walk on alone, in danger of being struck by lightning at any moment. Around him the lightning is striking here and there; in a minute it may strike him dead. But look! A mysterious hand is stretched over the traveler, covering and protecting him. Guarded by this loving hand, he can safely walk on through the thunderstorm. Because of that wonderful hand the lightning will not touch him. But look further. Like a linen cloth pierced by countless bullets, the hand which protects the traveler is being repeatedly struck by the lightning. This protecting hand is catching and intercepting the thunderbolts, which should fall on the traveler.

The meaning of this allegory is obvious. The thunderbolts of God's wrath were trying to pierce through us, the travelers. This is the whole point of Luke 12:4-5. But God's wrath never falls on us. God so loves and protects us that the very hairs of our head are numbered. This is the turth of Luke 12:6-7.

But what transforms this God of wrath into a God of love? No other than Jesus himself who "abruptly" joins these two themes together in these sayings. The works of Jesus authenticate his words. These two sayings were joined together by Jesus' bearing of God's wrath and his death on the cross. On every possible occasion in his sermons Jesus asked: ". . . and how is it written of the Son of man, that he should suffer many things and be treated with contempt?" (Mark 9:12). And we, who hear Jesus' sermon on the theme of fear and trust, must also hear his question: ". . . and how is it . . . ?" The conjunction "and" in the phrase "fear and trust" has an infinitely deep background. Fear and trust can be and have been united by "and"—Jesus made this possible by standing under the cross. If someone asks, "Where is the wrath of God?" we must always point to the cross of Jesus Christ, saying, "There I see God's wrath that strikes me."

When we think of Jesus telling of the five sparrows in order to teach us trust in God, we cannot check the tears. But the feeling is something more solemn than tears: let us call it *gratitude* for grace.

Chapter Eleven

The Pain of God
and Gospel History

I

A strange word is found in Paul's sermon at Athens: "And he
made from one every nation of men to live on all the face of the
earth, having determined allotted periods and the boundaries of
their habitation, that they should seek God, in the hope that they
might feel after him and find him" (Acts 17:26-27). Mankind is
divided into a variety of nations, and the scope of activity of each
nation has its own limitation, both in time and in space.

This is an obvious fact; there is no problem here. But what
inevitable connection is to be found between this fact and the
words "that they should seek God, in the hope that they might feel
after him and find him"? It seems to me that hitherto this question
has not been examined sufficiently. But here, I believe, we have a
clue to the important question as to how God's truth is related to
history.

Paul spoke these words in the Gentile city of Athens. The word
"Gentile" is used in contrast to "Jew." Now God's truth had gone
forth from Judea and was being proclaimed in a Gentile country.
How did this happen? According to Paul, it was because the Jews
"stumbled" at the truth of God, became "hardened," rejected it,
and were thus themselves "rejected" by God (Rom. 11:11, 15,
25). As a consequence, "through their trespass salvation has
come to the Gentiles . . . their trespass means riches for the world,
and . . . their failure means riches for the Gentiles" (Rom. 11:11-

12). Let us suppose that there had been no nation in the world but the Jewish people and that consequently no opposition between the Jews and the Gentiles had arisen. What would have happened then?

In that case, when the Jews became hardened to God's word, stumbled, and rejected it, the truth of God would have been completely taken away from the world. Since Gentiles as well as Jews existed, however, the truth of God which was rejected by the latter could be preserved by the former.

This is the reason why the division of nations has a necessary relationship to the discovery and preservation of the truth of God. The truth of God is nothing but the gospel. It is therefore clear that the gospel relates itself to world history for its own preservation. It means also that the gospel has its own history. We have now reached the concept of the history of the gospel, or what can be called "gospel history," which suggests the relationship between it and the historical realities of the world.[1]

II

Gospel history, seen in the contrast between Jews and Gentiles, presents a pattern for our thinking. We may safely say that this pattern can be developed further and used as a general principle. The historical development of the Christian church can be considered from the standpoint of gospel history.

According to Paul, gospel history includes historical elements, "allotted periods," and geographical elements, "boundaries of habitation." The contraposition between Judea and the Gentile world was a geographical confrontation, but it was also a historical contrast between the Old Testament and the New Testament periods. Bearing these two elements in mind, let us examine the related areas of gospel history.

The opposition between the Roman Catholic Church and the Protestant church reflects most clearly the pattern of gospel history as seen in the case of Judea and the Gentile world. Originally the Greco-Roman world was considered Gentile in contrast to Judea and was entrusted with preserving the gospel. The Greco-Roman church retained a positive significance for about five centuries, from the time of the primitive church to the establishment of the old Catholic Church. Calvin also believed that during this period of five hundred years the gospel retained its purity.[2] As this period passed, and the Roman Catholic Church gradually took its shape, however, it became "hardened" to the truth of the gospel and "stumbled." If the whole world had consisted of Roman Catholics, this "nation" would have lost the gospel, and consequently the whole world also would have lost it.

During this period of the decline of the gospel, a "nation" called the Germans had come into the picture with their "boundaries of habitation" outside of Rome. This German people had been despised as "barbarian," but God now entrusted the gospel to them. As Reinhold Seeberg says, the Reformation represents "Christianity in the understanding of the German spirit."[3] Luther puts it this way: "There is no nation so despised as the Germans. The Italians call us beasts; France, England and all other nations deride us. *Who ever knows what God wills for the Germans, or what he will do for them?*"[4] This leads us to believe in this connection that the preservation and spread of the gospel cannot be achieved simply by an individual, but only by a unit such as a race or a people. New possibilities of understanding the gospel are necessarily related to the "boundaries of habitation." According to Melanchthon, in the Middle Ages true churches existed only in those places where the doctrines of Augustine, Bernard, Tauler, or Wessel were taught.[5] But the gospel does not have a decisive significance if individuals alone hold its true understanding. The Reformation was accomplished, not through Wessel, but Luther, for it was actually through Luther that a national church was first organized. Here again gospel history is at work in the geographical and historical opposition between Rome and Germany, between the Middle Ages and modern times. The Reformation is not merely an event in the history of dogma. (According to Harnack, the Reformation even marks the end of the history of dogma!) In a deeper sense, the Reformation is an event in gospel history.

III

Theology ultimately is concerned with a view of God. A theology without a decisive view of God must be designated a half-baked theology. A view of God is concerned with the question of how the form of God is seen or apprehended. The characteristic utterance of theology is a creed. However, as far as the formulation of creeds is concerned, the view of God does not develop beyond that of the Greek and Roman churches. Although it certainly is of vital importance in regard to the view of faith, yet, on the whole, the Reformation inherited the view of God held by the Greek and Roman churches, and did not offer anything original of its own. It is true that the Reformers' view of God is more voluntaristic and personal than medieval theology; yet as far as it is expressed in the theology and creeds of the Reformation, their view of God does not have the decisive significance possessed by that of the Greek and Roman churches.

What then was the form of God apprehended by the Greco-Roman churches? This is expressed vividly in the Nicene and Athanasian creeds, which were the products of these churches. These creeds are the typical representation and crystallization of the church theology which lies in their background.[6]

Now the theology of the Greek and Roman churches became crystallized in the form of what is known as the immanent trinity. There God is apprehended as "three persons in one substance," *tres personae in una substantia*. Of course, the works of the economic trinity are expressed in the creed as creation, reconciliation, and sanctification, but these were only inherited from the primitive church, and not an original contribution of these churches.

The important matter for us now is the nature of the form of God described in the creed, particularly the nature of God which is understood in the concept of "essence." The word *persona* has a meaning as significant as "essence," but both of them have something in common as far as their nature is concerned. Because of its primitive associations, *persona* can be taken as a concept of personality; but, as a term used in the immanent trinitarianism, it is rather weak as a word for personality. So it would seem most fitting to replace it by "mode of existence," *tropos hyparxeos*, in the manner of the Cappadocian theologians. But the term "mode of existence" is an impersonal concept, and in that respect has the same disadvantage as the word "essence." As is well known, the word of vital importance in the Nicene Creed is *homo ousios*, "of one substance," of God the Father and God the Son. The

Nicene Creed focuses its attention on the implications of this word.

In the first section of the Athanasian Creed, the immanent trinity was given perfect expression. Here again one word, *substantia*, "essence," has decisive significance. *Neque confundentes personas; neque substantiam separantes:* "without confusion of persons; without separation of essence." The second section of this creed deals with Christology, and the word "essence" is again employed. *Deus ex substantia Patris:* "God who is from the essence of the Father."

It must be insisted that this concept of "essence" reflects a typical Greek way of thinking. It is true that the word "essence" is found in the New Testament. Hebrews 1:3 says that the Son "bears the very stamp of his nature." But this is the only reference in the Bible. It is commonly recognized that it was the Greek way of thinking which gave impetus to the adoption of this rare word, gave it a new significance, and caused the view of God to develop in the direction of this particular concept. We can trace the classical role played by the Greek way of thinking in the development of gospel history. It is almost impossible to overestimate its importance. The concept of the Trinity would never have found such a perfect and clear expression without the influence of Greek thought. We must gratefully follow the path of this truth.

But we must admit that the Greek way of thinking has its limitation as well as its positive significance. As discussed earlier, the description of God as "essence" lacks one decisive quality revealed in Scripture. "God in pain" which the prophet Jeremiah saw—this is decisive. Our task today is to advance one step beyond the position of the Greco-Roman churches while recognizing its place, yet recovering the biblical truth which they missed.

Is it possible, however, to expect the Greek way of thinking to make an advance in its view of God? Or can we expect it from the German mind? The achievements of these two "nations" are already attested in history. Yet, this one step has not been taken either by the Greek or by the German theology. No one denies the great contribution of Greek theology. However, the Greek mind is lacking in perception of the pain of God. In spite of Greek tragedy, this tragic spirit played no part in the formation of church theology. The Greek mind may be represented in Greek philosophy and Greek tragedy, but only the former seems to have made an impact upon the formation of church theology. The gospel may be called God's tragedy, but Greek tragedy never responded to it. This is probably because the content of Greek tragedy differs from that of the gospel—God's tragedy.

It is true that the German mind strikingly differs in character from that of the Greek. But the pain of God does not seem to have aroused the interest of the German mind in the strict sense of the words. Even in the case of Luther's concept of God, we cannot help saying, "Friend, not to that melody"! Certainly Luther possessed a sensitivity toward God's grace, but he did not grasp the meaning of grace as God's pain.

IV

When a "nation" discerns and worships God, it is important for us to know the *mind* of this "nation." This mind may be called a sense. It is not a thought, or a theory, or even a "spirit"! It is a sense, deeper than a spirit, more realistic. A "spirit" may belong to the upper, educated, and cultured classes, and may not belong to the common people. Thus it is often thought that a "spirit" must be implanted in the common people. But what is to be implanted does not represent the mind of the "nation." The mind of a "nation" is best represented by the common people. That which is possessed in unspoiled purity even by such humble people as the lower classes, the uneducated, the uncultured, and the non-religious—this is the real mind of a "nation." "Sense" is the word which expresses this mind most clearly. A sense is something possessed naturally, something retained without being taught, something that is passed on, as it were, by a nod. It is this sense which really determines the thought of a "nation." This sense plays a decisive role in the apprehension and worship of God.

How is this mind of a "nation" expressed? Needless to say, it is through its literature. But all literature does not necessarily express the mind of the common people. Some literature is acceptable only to the upper and cultured classes; some literature permeates even the lowest classes. What is important for us now is the latter. The literature of the common people, however, should not be low-grade reading material such as literature for the masses. It should be the literature which can maintain its loftiness as high as any other literature as an artistic expression of the mind of a nation, yet which can permeate the hearts of the common people—even of the lowest classes. The literature that fulfills such requirements is drama. Drama as literature belongs to the highest artistic expression of the mind of a nation, and at the same time, when presented as drama, permeates fully the people on the street corners. It is natural that the Greek mind is represented by both its philosophy and its tragedy.

In seeking for the Japanese mind, I believed that it should be found in the hearts of the common Japanese people; then I tried to find it in the classical dramas of Japan. I thought that the mind of the common people would be expressed in those classical dramas and that the sense, which is the premise of the Japanese way of thinking, would be revealed in the mind of the common people. The quest led me to the following conclusions.

First, the Japanese mind is living as the Japanese spirit in the so-called monism of light. At the same time, it is also living in the Japanese tragedies.[7] The tragedies are by no means the monism of light, but a light which contains darkness within itself. In order to display externally the Japanese spirit of the monism of light, the spirit of Japanese tragedy stands behind it as a background. Paradoxically, the spirit of tragedy is exalted most highly in Japan because the spirit of the monism of light is regarded as most powerful. The words of Matsuomaru in *The Temple School* show this relation quite pointedly: "Rejoice, my dear: our son has been of service to our lord."[8]

Second, what permeates the common people of Japan as their sense is the spirit of tragedy. The Japanese tragedies most deeply move the emotions of the common people—the uneducated, the uncultured, and the nonreligious. They are moved even to tears.

Third, Japanese tragedies are strikingly different in character from those of other countries. Whereas the latter are, for the most part, tragedies of incident or character, Japanese tragedy can be called the tragedy of personal relationships.

Fourth, these personal relationships are expressed by the particular Japanese word *tsurasa*.[9] (*Tsurasa* is neither bitterness nor sadness.) The depth of a truly Japanese man may be determined by his understanding of this *tsurasa*. According to the Japanese way of thinking, a man of depth, a man of understanding and intelligence, is one who understands *tsurasa*. One who does not understand *tsurasa* is shallow-minded and jejune—he is not like a true Japanese. The common people of the towns are more sensitive to *tsurasa* than the upper classes.

> The comparison and contrast of Japanese tragedies with those of Greece and other Western countries is a study of great importance which requires attention. Japanese tragedies are, of course, a hopeless confusion of good and bad, and some of them should be excluded from the above category. But most of the representative dramas, the best which have survived throughout history, belong to this category. This category of *tsurasa*, in my opinion, distinguishes Japanese tragedies from those of other countries. If Shakespeare's four great tragedies are compared with *The Temple School, Camp Kumagai, Benkei the Messenger,* and *The Sushi-monger,* the differences are immediately obvious.[10] Though both these groups of plays are tragedies, their nature is completely different. Shakespeare's tragedies are characterized by bitterness and sadness, but they do not have *tsurasa. Tsurasa* is the fundamental characteristic of Japanese tragedies. (I do not feel that Mr. Sadaji Yoshimura's *The Genealogy of Tragedies,* which is a study comparing Japanese and Western tragedies, treats the subject matter fully.)

V

Tsurasa, the basic principle in Japanese tragedy, is realized when one suffers and dies, or makes his beloved son suffer and die, for the sake of loving and making others live. Even though he tries hard to conceal and endure his agony, his cries filtering through his efforts are heard. When the Japanese playgoers hear these cries, they shed tears speechlessly. It is correct to say that nothing moves the mind of the Japanese as deeply as these spectacles.

The Japanese mind is represented by the mind of the common

people; the mind of the common people finds artistic expression in Japanese tragedy; the fundamental nature of Japanese tragedy is abridged as *tsurasa*. A more general term for *tsurasa* would be the word "pain." It is our conviction that the pain which is the only concern for Japanese tragedy corresponds most aptly with the pain of God, which is our main subject in this book. This is a most objective statement. Any impartial study of comparative literature would no doubt recognize this. Thus the Japanese mind, which had seen the deepest heart of his fellowman in pain, will come to see the deepest heart of the Absolute God in pain. Those of us who have been given the land of Japan as the "boundaries of habitation" will serve God with all our hearts, bearing the sense of pain as we attempt to comprehend the image and view of God. By so doing, one decisive aspect of God's nature, which was overlooked by the Greek churches, will be recovered by the churches of our country. Thus it becomes possible for another "boundary of habitation" to seek and find God.

However, the contrast between God of the Greek "essence" and God in pain is not merely the opposition of one relative view over against another relative view of God. The biblical view of God gives vital significance to the pain of God. To overlook this decisive matter means a misfortune for the church in the entire world.

VI

The above thoughts on gospel history in the Japanese matrix have been discussed on the basis of the geographical aspect, the "boundaries of habitation." But gospel history has at the same time the historical aspect of "allotted periods," as mentioned earlier. Let us now consider this aspect.

In every period of history, life and death, joy and pain, are intertwined. In some periods, life and joy are more pronounced than death and pain. Let us call these periods the age of life and the age of joy. There are also periods when death and pain are more pronounced than life and joy. Let us call these periods the age of death and the age of pain.

Because the gospel of the pain of God is eternal truth, man should be able to grasp it in any age. It is difficult, however, for us feeble men to understand this truth in the age of life and of joy.

In the periods in which Greek theology was born, or liberal theology emerged, it was difficult to comprehend the pain of God. But we are living in an age of death and pain.* The world today seems to be stretched out under pain, not under the great sky. Our age has spawned the saying "The span of life is twenty-five years."[11] What can we call it but an age of death?

Therefore one of the aspects of gospel history is its "allotted periods." One can best understand the pain of God in an age of pain. If we cannot comprehend this truth today, when shall we be able to? In our time, infinitely precious resources have poured into the making of our age of pain. This is the pain of the whole world. How can we possibly waste such precious resources? Although the efforts of the world may be reduced to nothingness, one thing will remain—the world has suffered today as never before. The agony of the world is a symbol of God's pain, and God's pain means the ultimate good tidings of the salvation of the world; these tidings are the truth of all truth.

The pain of God can be discerned most vividly in our age. However, it does not mean that the pain of God is a truth limited to our age; it is eternal truth for every age. But this eternal truth became discernible only in our age.

The pain of God can be discerned most vividly by the Japanese mind. However, it is not the truth for only one nation called Japan. It is a truth acceptable all over the world. But this universal truth would not have been discerned without Japan as its medium.

Those who see the heart of God most deeply see the reality of the human condition most deeply. And only the mind of God, which is deeper than any understanding, can solve the fundamental problem of human reality. The true knower of man (*Menschenkenner*) is the knower of God (*Gottes-kenner*).

VII

The foregoing remarks about the pain of God and the Japanese mind require the following reflections on our part.

First, in Japanese tragedy, as we have seen, *tsurasa*, or pain, is

---

* Translator's note: This was written during World War II.

experienced when one dies or sacrifices his beloved son in order to save another's life. But in this case the one saved is most precious to the one making the sacrifice.

The term "pain of God," however, has a double meaning. It represents the heart of God who loves the unlovable, on the one hand, and the heart of God who sacrifices his only beloved Son, on the other. The latter took place because of the former. The pain in Japanese tragedy, however, belongs only to the latter case. Even Japanese tragedy does not know the pain which is experienced by loving the unworthy, the unlovable, and even the enemy. (Even though the person to be loved may appear as an enemy—as, for example, in the case of Kan Shusai in *The Temple School*, Taira no Atsumori in *Camp Kumagai*, or Taira no Koremori in *The Sushi-monger*—yet all these are eminently worthy of respect.) Consequently, pain in Japanese tragedy has only one side of the pain of God, lacking the other. (See Rom. 5:7-8.)

Second, man's sensitivity toward pain retains selfish motive and illusion, although it serves the pain of God by understanding it. This disobedient human sensitivity must be overcome by God's pain which sanctions it and uses it for his service. Our previous discussion on the analogy of pain can be proved to be true here.

Third, man's sensitivity toward pain becomes productive and truthful only when it serves God's pain. Sensitivity toward pain, separated from God, is in danger of losing its ethical implications. "Play" (*Spiel*) can mean "drama" or "game." It is fatal when the sensitivity toward pain is used in terms of games. Games do not have ethical connotations. The Japanese common people have sensitivity toward pain and yet have a tendency to disassociate themselves from ethics. We must regretfully admit this fact and give serious thought to it. This tendency may be ascribed to the fact that the sensitivity toward pain has not yet reached the point of serving the pain of God. The pain of God alone makes it possible to intensify pain which is the basis of ethics.

Chapter Twelve

The Pain of God
and Eschatology

I

" '. . . what will be the sign of your coming and of the close of the age?' " (Matt. 24:3). This is the quest for eschatology in a more original sense of the word—the quest for Christ's second coming and the end of the world. Jesus' response to this quest, therefore, should be regarded as the ultimate answer to this quest for eschatology. It is for this reason that Matthew 24 is considered as a decisive section in the Scriptures for our consideration of eschatology.

What are the signs of the End according to Jesus? His answer is found in verse 14: " 'And this gospel of the kingdom will be preached throughout the whole world, as a testimony to all nations; and then the end will come.' " The signs of the End are to be found in that the gospel has been proclaimed to the uttermost part of the world. The appearance of the antichrist, war, famine, earthquake, and the like are not to be taken as signs of the End. They are "the beginning of the sufferings" (vs. 8). They are not the decisive events. But how these clear words of Jesus have been obscured! How often have these events been considered the signs of the End! " 'The kingdom of God is not coming with signs to be observed' " (Luke 17:20). In spite of this clear teaching of Jesus, how often have signs of God's Kingdom been sought in observable events. These errors have thrown eschatology into irreparable confusion. Today this issue requires radical clarification. The End should be understood only in light of the gospel. All mistaken eschatologies have been fatally conceived and discussed apart from the gospel.

The coming of the Kingdom of God is the coming of the rule of God. How can his rule be achieved? It is not by power, but by the love of God. Speaking more concretely, the love of God *is* his gospel. Therefore the rule of God is realized only when the gospel is spread throughout the entire world, as the air encircles the globe. A complete diffusion of the gospel—this is the sign of the End. The last day is the time when the world comes to its end and the ultimate is realized. At this consummation, all unsolvable questions will be answered, all doubts will be resolved, and all tears will be wiped away. " 'In that day you will ask nothing of me' " (John 16:23). This means the salvation of the world. Only the gospel can relieve the burdens of the world and bring salvation.

Only the diffusion of the gospel, the salvation of the world, has significance for the end. This is the heart of eschatology. All other things, especially the "visible events," are *adiaphora* (matters of insignificance). The weakness of those concerned with the "signs" lies in their obsession with *adiaphora*, apart from the heart of eschatology. ". . . they have a zeal for God, but it is not enlightened" (Rom. 10:2).

II

According to Jesus, tribulation will appear at the end of the world. (See Matt. 24:21 and 1 Cor. 7:26.) It will be a "great" tribulation, such "as has not been from the beginning of the world until now, no, and never will be." The end will be the days of "tribulation" (Mark 13:19). What is the relation of the tribulation to the diffusion of the gospel which is the heart of eschatology —is there a natural connection between them? Here lies the signal question of eschatology.

What is the essence of the gospel? It is the cross of Christ, the pain of God, or it is God's tribulation, if one is permitted to use this term. The End will come when the gospel is diffused, but this also implies the diffusion of the message of his tribulation. It is natural that the world will bear suffering as a witness to the diffusion of the gospel which is God's "tribulation." The words Jesus spoke suddenly in his eschatological discourse, " 'But first he must suffer many things and be rejected by this generation' " (Luke 17:25), become intelligible in light of this concept. The diffusion of the gospel of God's pain necessitates the diffusion of the world's pain; the fulfillment of the salvation of the world presupposes the suffering of the Son of Man. The necessary connection between the pain of God and eschatology is thus established.

Because the End depends on the diffusion of the gospel, the world will not cease until its suffering, corresponding to God's pain, is diffused. Because suffering is not diffused, the End has not yet come. When suffering is diffused, the End will come. This is the criterion for the arrival of the End. Therefore, all attempts to seek criteria in "signs" are to be rejected. " 'But of that day and hour no one knows . . .' " (Matt. 24:36).

The various signs accompanying the End should not be our concern. We must see through these events the complete manifestation of God's pain as the redemption of mankind. "Now when these things begin to take place, look up and raise your heads, because your redemption is drawing near" (Luke 21:28).

Although we cannot know the exact day or hour, we are permitted to know when the time is approaching. " 'Look at the fig tree, and all the trees; as soon as they come out in leaf, you see for yourselves and know that the summer is already near. So also, when you see these things taking place, you know that the kingdom of God is near' " (Luke 21:29-31). When there will be "upon the earth distress of nations" (vs. 25), we will be required to perceive the omens of the time. " 'Wherever the body is, there the eagles will be gathered together' " (Matt. 24:28).

When the twenty-two-year-old Luther interrupted his student life to enter the monastery in Erfurt, he "was surrounded by the fear of death and unrest."[1] At that time Luther felt surrounded by death as though he were walled in (*circumvallatus*). After passing through this "time of death," he felt himself entered into a "golden age" (*aureum saeculum*), and believed that the last day (*der junsttag*) would follow.[2] The suffering of this generation certainly is greater than that of the plague in the sixteenth century.

> In the eschatological discourse, a careful distinction is made between the tribulation of man (*thripsis*, Matt. 24:21) and the suffering of Christ (*pathein*, Luke 17:25), following the New Testament usage. This shows the qualitative difference between the pain of God and that of man. In spite of this qualitative difference, it is doubtful whether "tribulation" and "suffering" can be strictly distinguished in practice. Mere verbal distinction results in a game of words and becomes abstract. For our present purpose we should learn through these two words the similarity and qualitative difference between the pain of God and that of man.

III

Man's pain is intended to witness to the pain of God. When man's pain is not related to God's saving work, it reflects the wrath of God. The "tribulation" at the last day implies God's wrath (Luke 21:23), judgment (vs. 22), and man's destruction (1 Thess. 5:3). If this reality of God's wrath is ever to be used as a witness to his pain, it is because of his grace. As we have discussed in the chapter "Service for the Pain of God," the pain of the world is healed by being made a witness to the pain of God. It is our prayer that we shall be of service to God even in the "tribulation" of the last days.

Love rooted in the pain of God causes his pain to diffuse. The Son of Man "with great power and glory" will appear "after that tribulation" (Mark 13:24, 26). This event is the fulfillment of the love of God which is the victory of the pain of God. By this love, the rule of God, that is, his Kingdom, comes.

As we saw above, love rooted in God's pain comes intensively to those of us who have faith in him, delivering us from all tribulation. Even when "that day come[s] upon you suddenly like a snare," believers will be able to pray that they "may have the strength to escape all these things that will take place" (Luke 21:34, 36).

Here we see that the three orders of God's love are united and correlated with one another in eschatology. The wrath of God, the first order, though basically revealed as darkness, is upheld and used as a witness to his pain. The pain of God, the second order, develops into the love rooted in it. Thus the love of God, the third order, delivers the believer from his wrath, the first order.

IV

Eschatology is not a partial truth occupying the last chapter of dogmatics. The eschatological is of such a nature as to determine the whole structure of the gospel and faith. We must now consider this aspect.

The pain of God, as grace conquering sinners, provides a complete solution for the forgiveness of sins. This is the doctrine of reconciliation. Only by this grace does God resolve all things. Only by faith in this grace alone do we enter perfect salvation. "Grace alone," "faith alone"—such familiar evangelical expressions reflect this truth. This is the viewpoint of the "theological axiom." By looking at this truth alone, we find that the Ultimate, the End, has arrived by the coming of Jesus Christ who is the personification of pain. (The Gospel of John is known to emphasize this part.) But the pain of God necessarily develops into love rooted in the pain of God. That is, grace as the forgiveness of sins develops into grace as the sanctification of forgiven sinners. Speaking of the "theological reality," this is the doctrine of sanctification or redemption. In reality this sanctification remains incomplete and unfulfilled. In other words, this reality is unresolved. Pointing to this unresolved condition is God's love, the development of his pain, or the "yearning of [God's] heart," which is described as being withheld in Isaiah 63:15. This unresolved condition is due to the continued disobedience of our world in this broken order of creation. By looking at this truth alone, therefore, the Ultimate, the End, becomes a hope in the future.

Now the basic structure of the gospel is found in the unity of these two viewpoints mentioned above—the theological axiom and the theological reality. Here the resolved and the unresolved are fused together while retaining their own characteristics. The following words of Paul express this relationship splendidly: "Not that I have already obtained this or am already perfect; but I press to make it my own, because Christ Jesus has made me his own" (Phil. 3:12). The Ultimate, the End, is conceived as a present reality, while, at the same time, pointing to the future.

The tension arising from the fusion of these two contradictory truths is eschatological in the deepest sense of the word. The answer to this insolvable contradiction can only be sought in hope. The tension which faith holds continues on with the hope for a final vindication at the end of the world. The faith living in this reality—the resolved within the unresolved—is truly eschatological. Inasmuch as this structure is basic to the gospel, the eschatological content is also basic to the gospel.[3]

The pain of God is an all-embracing principle. When fused with this pain, eschatology also acquires an all-embracing nature. It is obvious that our eschatology fundamentally differs from that of "principle of negation" or "theology of rejection."

Chapter Thirteen

Conclusion

I

It has been our sincere desire to see deeply into the heart of God, by following the example of Jeremiah. This desire has been fulfilled by seeing the pain of God, as did Jeremiah. We were astonished to find the inner heart of God as pain.

In our closing chapter, we must mention one more astonishing fact: we were allowed to see the pain of God. While it is astonishing to see the inner heart of God as pain (content), it is more astonishing for us to be allowed to see this pain of God (method). "He who sees the face of God will die!" Then how is it possible for a man who saw the heart of God to live? The pain of God is the "wisdom of death." We cannot see God's pain without risking death. Without this risk, the "theology" of the pain of God cannot be established. Seeing is "knowing"; without knowing no scholarship can be established. If a seeker of knowledge must inevitably die, scholarship can never be realized.

In order to establish the theology of the pain of God, there must be a particular provision for rescuing "seeing" and "knowing." I found such a provision in the words of Exodus 33:22: " '. . . and while my glory passes by I will put you in a cleft of the rock, and I will cover you with my hand until I have passed by . . .' " If we see the glory of God directly, its brilliance burns our eyes, and we shall die. " '. . . you cannot see my face; for man shall not see me and live' " (Exod. 33:20).

God reveals his glory by covering us with his own hand, allowing us to escape death. Although we cannot see his glory directly, we are allowed to see his hand covering us. This sheltering hand manifests his will to save us from death. Is there anything deeper in the heart of God than his will for salvation? This will for salvation is far deeper than the desire to reveal his glory directly. The sheltering hand of God is his deepest and most essential nature. His will for salvation is manifested in the person of Jesus Christ as his pain. The pain of God reveals himself while saving us. The glory of the cross reflects the radiance of his face.

Since the heart of God had not been fully revealed to Moses, God said, " '. . . then I will take away my hand, and you shall see my back; but my face shall not be seen' " (Exod. 33:23).

Since the heart of God was revealed to Paul through Jesus Christ, it became possible for Paul to have hope of seeing his glory face to face. "And we all, with unveiled face, beholding the glory of the Lord, are being changed into his likeness from one degree of glory to another . . ." (2 Cor. 3:18). "For now we see in a mirror dimly, but then face to face" (1 Cor. 13:12).

For the wisdom of the new covenant, God is revealed in his sheltering hand for our salvation. "Theology of glory" can be understood only through "theology of the cross." God's love can be understood only on the basis of his pain. His glory is the radiance of the cross; his love is the victory of his pain. Our task then is to comprehend the depth of Christ's love as God's pain.

This comprehension is the true knowledge and wisdom, witnessing to theology which serves for God's glory. ". . . that according to the riches of his glory he may grant you to be strengthened with might through his Spirit in the inner man, and that Christ may dwell in your hearts through faith; that you, being rooted and grounded in love, may have power to comprehend with all the saints what is the breadth and length and height and depth, and to know the love of Christ which surpasses knowledge, that you may be filled with all the fulness of God" (Eph. 3:16-19). The power of this love alone enables us to know Christ's immeasurable love.

We must be astonished both by the content (the pain of God) and by the method (that which establishes the theology of the pain of God). The content (the pain of God) enables the method (man's knowledge) to establish theology. This is why the "content" must be stated in the prolegomena of this theology.

II

"Theology of the pain of God" dares to speak about the matters related to the pain of God. We must speak about the things of God by using our human experience. This is essentially the meaning of "witness." Witness is possible only when such an experience is given in human language, not in God's terms, for our witness is intended for all mankind. In witnessing, men's affairs serve the things of God. In witnessing to God's pain, man's pain serves this purpose.

In our discussion, the pain of man played a positive role which is natural in the light of the theme of this book—"*theology* of the pain of God." It should be noted again that the pain of God *gives* meaning and value to human suffering.

We must admit that human suffering is able to serve in comprehending the meaning of God's pain, but human suffering does not have this value within itself; it is only given to man by God's pain. The surpassing grace of God's pain makes human suffering valuable and precious.

We recognize that of all our spiritual experiences, pain is the deepest and most precious. Thus, as the saying goes, it is profitless to talk with "those who have not eaten their bread with tears." This also is why tragedy is recognized as the essence of literature. Further, from the standpoint of the Bible, it is the experience of pain which turns men to God. ". . . in their distress they seek me . . ." (Hos. 5:15). "Before I was afflicted I went astray; but now I keep thy word" (Ps. 119:67).

But human pain itself is valueless, being the fallen reality of creation. "All art"—including tragedy—"originated with the fall of Adam and Eve."[1] Even the most precious and beautiful creations of man remain ultimately imperfect and dark.

The gospel is the tidings of salvation which remove and resolve this ultimate darkness. The pain of man corresponds with that of God which is the content of the gospel. The pain of man which is basically the reality of darkness is allowed to enter into the "light" for witnessing to the tidings of salvation. This change into light from darkness is possible only by man's response to God's action. This change is determined not by the immanent value of human beings but by the transcendent grace of God. This transcendence saves the contradiction of immanence. Japanese tragedy has a greater value than Greek tragedies and others because its content corresponds more closely to God's pain—tragedy of God. Judging from a purely literary standpoint, the value of Japanese tragedy cannot be compared with others. It may not be so simple to advocate the superiority of Japanese tragedy; and it is even conceivable to receive opposite opinion of Japanese tragedy. (We must take into consideration the fact that Japanese tragedy has never been recognized on the stage of world literature.) Judging from the context, we have to uphold Japanese tragedy in the theological area because any fair comparative study of literature must recognize that *tsurasa*, the heart of Japanese tragedy, corresponds most closely to the pain of God. For our purpose, the significance of Japanese tragedy is not so much in its literary value as in its theological one. This theological value comes from that of transcendence.

If this principle be established, we are permitted to think freely of the relationship between the pain of God and that of man. We may think not only that man's pain is the symbol of God's pain, but contrariwise, that God's pain is the symbol of man's pain.

> "But there is something else that hits me hard, and that is the expression on the face of a wounded man enduring violent pain. His face, filthy with dirt, unshaven, and emaciated, would gradually come to resemble in its struggle with pain, as night followed day, the expression on the face of Christ you see in pictures."[2]

III

"Scholar"—*schola* in Latin—is derived from the Greek *schole*, meaning "freedom from occupation." But "leisure"[3] is not the only meaning of *schole*. "Freedom from occupation" means that the scholar maintains some distance from mundane affairs, thereby allowing desirable environment for study. Without this freedom from occupation, learning cannot be realized, as a rule.

The theology of the pain of God can be pursued only when we participate in it through our own suffering. Yet our pain deprives us of all "freedom." Although "freedom" is essential for learning, the theology of the pain of God is pursued only by the medium of pain which deprives us of this "freedom." How can such a theology be established? This theology can exist only through the power of its object: the pain of God. The pain of God—the gospel —aims at removing and resolving the pain which results when we are taken down from our ivory tower. Pain shakes the very foundation of our existence, yet God sustains those of us whose foundation is shaking, when we participate in his pain.

The theology of the pain of God is pursued only by our own pain. This means that we place ourselves in an emotional situation where we are taken down from our ivory tower. However, the theology of the pain of God is strictly "theology," which is rational. We can be thoroughly rational and at the same time completely in the emotional situation. This is because the object of our reason redeems our emotional situation.

We are saved by the love rooted in the pain of God. Only those who are embraced by this love of God can pursue the theology of the pain of God. Only the conqueror of pain can understand pain.

There are two kinds of people in the world: those who experience pain, but do not understand it, and those who understand pain, but are not experiencing it. These two types of people can be untroubled: The former is subjectively untroubled; the latter is objectively untroubled. But the "study of pain" cannot be pursued by these people.

In Kant's terms, the former lacks form while the latter lacks substance. Those who can understand pain must also actually experience it in order to establish the theology of the pain of God. The study of pain can be pursued only by such a person. But he will perish at that moment. Because he is human, he will perish physically and spiritually the moment he experiences pain with the ability to understand it. Only by the sustaining hands of transcendental grace at this moment can the study of pain be pursued. "When I thought, 'My foot slips,' thy steadfast love, O Lord, held me up" (Ps. 94:18). This steadfast love is love rooted in the pain of God.

IV

My prayer night and day is that the gospel of love rooted in the pain of God may become real to all men. All human emptiness will be filled if this gospel is known to every creature, since the answer to every human problem lies in the gospel. Therefore I pray, "May thou, O Lord, make known to all men thy love rooted in the pain of God." The greatest joy and thanksgiving comes from the knowledge that this prayer is being granted and that step by step this gospel is becoming real to mankind.

We must emphatically note here that the gospel, in making itself known to man, should retain its characteristic of being "outside the gate" (Heb. 13:12). Jesus suffered "outside the gate" in order to cleanse the people by his own blood, just as the sacrificial offering was burnt "outside the camp" in Old Testament days. We must therefore go forth to him outside the camp, bearing abuse for him (Heb. 13:11-13). In order for the gospel to become real in our world, it must not enter "inside the gate"—into the center of the city; it must remain "outside." If the gospel loses its characteristic of being "outside" in our world, it is no longer the gospel and is not even worthy of our consideration. The theology of the pain of God, if true to itself, must retain this characteristic of being "outside." It should never become a so-called "dominant" theology. ". . . we have become, and are now, as the refuse of the world, the offscouring of all things" (1 Cor. 4:13).

APPENDIX

JEREMIAH 31:20 AND ISAIAH 63:15

"Is Ephraim my dear son? is he a pleasant child? for since I spake against him, I do earnestly remember him still: therefore my bowels are troubled for him; I will surely have mercy upon him, saith the LORD" (Jer. 31:20, K.J.V.).

"Look down from heaven, and behold from the habitation of thy holiness and of thy glory: where is thy zeal and thy strength, the sounding of thy bowels and of thy mercies toward me? are they restrained?" (Isa. 63:15, K.J.V.).

I

Ever since this strange word struck me, I have meditated on it night and day. It was literally a strange word for me. My astonishment at the mystery of this word was deepened more and more as I discovered its relationship to Isaiah 63:15.

The word is translated as "my bowels are troubled" in Jeremiah 31:20 and as "the sounding of thy bowels and of thy mercies" in Isaiah 63:15. Let us examine the meaning of this word as objectively as possible.

Two Hebrew words used in the phrases *hamu me ai* ("my bowels are troubled"), Jeremiah 31:20, and *hamon me eika* ("mercies"), Isaiah 63:15, consist of the same noun, *me aim*, and the same verb, *hamah*. The noun means "bowel," indicating the seat of the heart or the heart itself. There is no problem with this word. The verb *hamah* requires careful attention. It means: (1) "to sound" (e.g., the noise of the sea, Isaiah 17:12; Jeremiah 5:22; the roar of beasts, as in Isaiah 59:11; Psalm 59:6; the clamor of heathen nations, Psalm 46:6), and (2) the condition of man's heart (and of God's!). We must consider this second usage.[1]

What kind of condition of the heart are we speaking about? Each biblical usage of this term will certainly help us to clarify its meaning. Only the two passages cited above (Jer. 31:20 and Isa. 63:15) use the term in reference to God; all the other passages refer to man. The prophets, psalmists, and others describe the condition of their own hearts by this term.

"My anguish, my anguish! I writhe in pain! Oh, the walls of my heart! My heart is *beating wildly* [*homeh*] . . ." (Jer. 4:19).

"Therefore my heart *moans* [*yehemah*] for Moab like a flute, and my heart *moans* like a flute for the men of Kirheres . . ." (Jer. 48:36).

"Evening and morning and at noon I utter my complaint and *moan* [*ehemeh*]. . ." (Ps. 55:17).

"Therefore my soul *moans* [*yehemu*] like a lyre for Moab, and my heart for Kirheres" (Isa. 16:11).

". . . I groan because of the *tumult* [*ne hamah*] of my heart" (Ps. 38:8).

". . . for nought are they in *turmoil*" (Ps. 39:6).

". . . O my soul . . . why are you *disquieted* within me?" (Pss. 42:5, 11; 43:5).

"I think of God, and I *moan* . . ." (Ps. 77:3).

"My beloved put his hand to the latch, and my heart was *thrilled* [*hamu*] within me" (Song of Sol. 5:4).

The above examples (with the exception of the Song of Solomon) give us some definite impressions of the meaning of the word *hamah*, which the prophets and psalmists intended to show. The impression from these passages in regard to the condition of man's heart provides us with a clue to understanding the condition of God's heart as described by the same word. (It is only through the grace of God that we are allowed to perceive his inner heart by an analogy of the condition of man's heart. Just as in the parable of the Prodigal Son in the relations between the father and his son, we are permitted to know the heart of God by means of events that happen in the world of men.)

A meaning of the word *hamah* similar to the above-cited passages can also be found in Jeremiah 31:20 where Jeremiah applied the word to God. Jeremiah must have seen in God the same condition of the heart which the prophets and psalmists themselves experienced. What kind of condition? The pain! The pain of God!

We cannot possibly perceive what the "pain of God" is. But we know the meaning of "pain" experienced in our human heart. Through this experience, God tries to reveal to us what is taking place in his heart—just as Jesus revealed our "Heavenly Father's" love to us by human analogy known to us as the father's love toward his prodigal son. This revelation is by the mercy of God, and not to be explained as the Thomist "analogy of existence."

Thus Jeremiah used the word "pain" in its most precise meaning to describe the love of God toward sinners. Only this word could express the severest struggle of God's love which Jeremiah saw.

Any attempt to soften the meaning of this word would result in losing the significance of the fact to which the word points. Such an interpretation as a "sympathetic feeling," *Sympathieempfindung*, by Gesenius, or "mercy," *Erbarmen*, by Cassell, loses the decisive meaning of the word. God's reality, as seen by Jeremiah, is not only grasped but rather suffocated by an interpretation such as "sympathy" or "mercy." (Here one recalls Feuerbach who sneered at the doctrine of the incarnation as a demonstration of God's sympathetic and human-like tears, or Nietzsche who scoffed at "kindness and good will" as the worst kind of morality springing from the Christian concept of God!)

A sensitivity toward God, not an aptitude for linguistic analysis, is required for our understanding of the term in question. Let us listen to two witnesses who were most sensitive toward grace: Luther, the translator, and Calvin, the commentator.

Luther translates Jeremiah 31:20 as follows: *Darum bricht mir mein Herz gegen ihn, dass ich mich sein erbarmen muss.* The words *mein Herz bricht mir* may be paraphrased in German as *ich empfinde den heftigsten Schmerz* ("I feel a very severe pain"). The translations "my bowels are troubled for him" (k.j.v.) and *waga harawata . . . itamu* ("my bowels are in pain," Japanese

Literary Version) agree with Luther's on the whole. *Espeusa,* in the Septuagint, and *conturbata,* in the Vulgate, suggest the similar rendering, though the degree of their emphasis may differ slightly. The above-cited Cassell's dictionary gives *klagen, jammern* ("grieve," "wail"), for the meaning of the word.

Calvin's following comment is equally as important as Luther's above translation. "In this passage, God is grieving over the Israel on whom his great mercy had no effect, for they had been adopted as his sons by his grace. By their ingratitude, however, they wasted God's grace. God asks himself what kind of people Israel had been. . . . Ephraim was unworthy of any respect and could never be an object of God's love. . . . They were also unworthy of any mercy because of their intended disregard of their adoption . . . These sons were not precious, worthy of respect, or lovable . . . God was unable to love them because of their wicked character. They were evil-minded sons, disobedient sons, and sons who tor-- tured their father, hurt his feelings, and filled him with sorrows. . . . Because their wickedness and corruption were so great, we won- der whether God can still endure them. We are drawn back to the fountain of God's great mercy in that he can even forgive them because he first chose them . . ."

Calvin now discusses the passage "my bowels are troubled."

"God enhances the reconciling grace further by saying, 'there- fore my bowels are troubled for him; I will surely have mercy upon him.' Here God attributes human feelings to himself; for our bowels are shaken and roar under extraordinary 'pain' (*dolor*), and we sigh and groan deeply under the pressure of great sorrow. God, therefore, expresses his feelings as an affectionate father: 'my bowels are troubled' [literally "roar"] in accepting his people back in his grace. Such a thing does not properly belong to God. God's nature is to feel this way, but he expresses himself *imperfectly* in terms of our human ignorance, knowing no other way to communicate the greatness of his love toward us."[2]

Both Luther and Calvin discerned the "pain of God" in Jere- miah 31:20. "Pain" (*Schmerz*) by Luther and "pain" (*dolor*) by Calvin are not to be considered sentimental. In fact, Luther and Calvin were probably far less sentimental than most people. "Sentimental" is not the word for the above quotations, for the "pain of God" is the severest experience we know of.

Those who call people who advocate the "pain of God" "sentimentalists" will in turn end in reading passages like Luke 15 and Romans 5 sentimentally!

Let us quote some examples from several commentators who basically agree with Calvin:

"Yahweh's words against Ephraim are not only of threat but also of punishment by the act of his judgment. God must think of Ephraim as his precious son, if he still thinks of him in spite of his due punishment. This attitude does not arise from Ephraim's behavior or from his efforts to please God by his obedience and loyalty, but it comes from God's unchanging love, trying not to lose his son, so much so that God suffers pain on account of Ephraim, his son."[3]

"In this beautiful soliloquy of Yahweh, the prophet does not shrink from the boldest anthropomorphism. Whenever the name of Ephraim passes His lips, the tender memory revives in His heart. True, it is with horror and with threatening that He must speak of his conduct, yet the mention of his name even in anger revives all the ancient love. Moved to amazement by the paradox of His conflicting emotions, He asks Himself the reason. Is it because Ephraim is His darling child that, in spite of all his ingratitude and disobedience, the old affection surges up irrepressibly at every mention of his name?"[4]

"Yahweh wonders how he still finds love for Ephraim in his heart."[5]

Calvin, Keil, Peake, Giesebrecht, Menge, and others interpret verse 20 as: "Is Ephraim my dear son? Is he my darling child?" (r.s.v.). This translation by these scholars and the American Standard Version is preferred to "Is not . . . ?" as found in the Japanese Version and Luther's translation. Giesebrecht's rendering—"As often as I am angry against him"—is more suggestive than "as often as I speak against him." Menge also translates "as often as I threaten him."

The following words of Peake on the book of Jeremiah as a whole are helpful in understanding this portion of the text. "We watch him [Jeremiah] as he staggers and totters under the weight of the cross to which God had doomed him, a lifelong agony for the sin and sorrow of his people, for God's pain and his own."[6]

Judging from the above comments, there is no doubt that Jeremiah 31:20 speaks of the "pain of God." This "pain of God" is not a mere qualifying word for the power and intensity of his love. The "pain of God" is different from "love of God." That is, the "pain of God" reflects his love toward those turning against it. The pain of God enfolds within itself his immediate love, working as a medium which must be rejected because of human sin. It is therefore on a higher plane than his "love," and witnesses to the "love of the cross." The "love of the cross" is poured upon those turning against God's immediate love which functions as law. The "pain of God"—the gospel—is love which is witnessed to, yet revealed, outside of the law. Both the "pain of God" and "love of the cross" reflect love which is poured on us by *cancelling* our sin of *rejecting* God's love—it is the absolutely affirmative love shown in these double negatives. Man can turn against the immediate "love of God" but not against the "pain of God," the love of the cross.

We must think deeply about the result of being captured in the "pain of God"—the love of God who accepts as his own sinners who are turning their backs on him. The complete victory of "God's pain" over sinners takes place at that time. Christ's complete victory—the resurrection—takes place in sinners when they can no longer turn against the love of his cross. The victory of "God's pain" is his love which has pierced through the pain—that is, "love rooted in the pain of God." The resurrection of Christ which conquers death on the cross is his victory. Thus the "pain of God" is at once the "love of God." The death of Christ is at once his resurrection. Just as the other side of Christ's death is his resurrection, the other side of God's "pain" is his love.[7]

Now we must turn our attention to Isaiah 63:15.

II

As indicated above, the terms "the yearning of thy heart" (R.S.V.) of Isaiah 63:15 and "my bowels are troubled" (A.V.) of Jeremiah 31:20 are derived from the same word. The concept of the "pain of God" was clarified in the above discussion of Jeremiah 31:20. Turning our attention to Isaiah 63:15, we find that this same term is used definitely to indicate the love of God, not the pain of God. Ever since the Septuagint rendered the Hebrew word by the Greek *eleos*—which obviously means God's love—all translations and commentaries have followed its interpretation. The English rendering of "compassion" and the Japanese *renbin* would be proper as equivalent terms. Just as the meaning of *hamah* in Jeremiah 4:19 can be derived from its equivalent, "I writhe in pain," so the meaning of *hamah* in Isaiah 63:15 can be derived from its equivalent, "compassion." A similar insight can be drawn from the unusual usage in verse 16—of calling God "Redeemer." There is no doubt that the term *hamah* in Isaiah 63:15 implies God's "love." In this instance, however, God's "love" is not his immediate love which men can easily turn against, but his "intent" love as described in verse 16: ". . . though Abraham does not know us and Israel does not acknowledge us; thou, O Lord, art our Father."

This investigation shows that the term *hamah* implies "pain" and "love," interchangeably or simultaneously. God's love— which is poured out on those rebelling against him—"God's pain"—immediately implies his "love" completely conquering those rebels. The word *hamah*, meaning simultaneously both pain and love, is not simply a mystery of language, but also a mystery of grace. That is, the mystery of grace means that the Christ of the cross is at the same time the Christ of the resurrection, and justification is at once sanctification.

> It is interesting that a word with a double meaning helps us to understand the concrete nature of a fact. A striking example of this can be found in Kant's philosophical use of the word "transcendental." As is well known, this term is basic to Kant's philosophy; however, it was traditionally interpreted as a priori. Recently, it has been claimed that the term strictly means "transcendental." This claim is right, but the essence of Kant's epistemology can best be comprehended by the combination of these two meanings, "a priori" and "transcendental," into one word, the German *transzendental*.

It has become clear that the Hebrew word *hamah* means pain and love simultaneously. Because *hamah* also means "love," we should not quickly conclude that in Jeremiah 31:20 the term merely modifies the power of God's love. The eleven above examples include almost all the cases where the word is used to describe the condition of a man's heart, but in ten of these cases (excluding Song of Sol. 5:4) it is used only to describe pain and not in the sense of love. All commentators admit this. The clause "my heart is beating wildly," in Jeremiah 4:19, implies "pain," as we have seen, in its equation with "I writhe in pain" (Vulgate: *doleo*; K.J.V.: "I am pained"; Jewish Version: "I am twisted with pain"). Keil interprets the term as "grief," while Peake translates it as "anguish." Calvin interprets "my bowels shall sound," of Isaiah 16:11 (K.J.V.), as *dolor*, "pain";[8] and Delitzsch reads *Schmerz*, "pain."[9] Calvin also interprets "I utter my complaint and moan," of Psalm 55:17 as *dolor*, "pain,"[10] and Briggs renders the same by "pain."[11] Calvin again interprets "moan" of Psalm 77:3 as *dolor*, "pain."[12] Thus in most passages *hamah* is rendered by "pain."

It is questionable whether "my heart was thrilled" (Song of Sol. 5:4, R.S.V., which was excluded from our previous discussion) means "love." Checking various translations of this passage, we find that Luther renders *erzittern*, "tremble violently, shudder"; Staerk renders *beben*, "shiver"; Kautzsch renders *wallen*, "be agitated"; King James Version renders "to move"; and only the Jewish Version renders "to yearn for." In this passage, it may mean "tumult," as in Psalm 38:8. Even if the rendering of "love" be accepted, this is only one instance out of eleven. We must therefore admit that *hamah* is almost always used for "pain" rather than for "love."

Jeremiah 31:20 should be understood primarily in the sense of pain which, as we have discussed, is related to "love" in the mystery of grace. ("I will surely have mercy on him," at the end of verse 20, is relevant here.) Certainly "pain" is "love," but this love ought to be rooted in pain. The rendering of Jeremiah 31:20 merely as a modification of love such as "yearning for," by seeing only the immediate "love" and not taking into account the "pain," reveals not only a lack of philological perception, but also a failure to understand the grace itself implied by this word. Is not this the work of Satan, who prompted Peter to say, ". . . Lord! This shall never happen to you" (Matt. 16:22, R.S.V.)? Jeremiah 31:20 must be interpreted as God's "pain." (The Septuagint and the Vulgate are correct.) It is a mystery corresponding to grace which makes the term serve to indicate clearly God's "love" in Isaiah 63:15. Our study shows that not only exposition but also translation of the Bible is a confession of faith.

In order to confirm the above expository study, let us consider the place of Jeremiah 31:20 in the entire context of the book. External evidence suggests that chapter 31 (possibly chapter 30) belongs to the closing section of the entire 52 chapters of the book and that the date of the chapter is after the fall of Jerusalem in 586 B.C. This was toward the end of Jeremiah's prophetic work which began with his call (626 B.C.) and ended with the Babylonian Captivity (586 B.C.). (It is interesting that Delitzsch, Orelli, and others connect 31:15-22 with 40:1 and interpret these passages as "God's utterance" to Jeremiah after he passed Ramah on his way to the Babylonian Captivity. I cannot accept Peake's position of separating this particular passage from chapter 31 and of relegating it to an earlier period.) When the entire chapter 31 is seen as Jeremiah's final words, the truth revealed therein is of ultimate significance. Chapter 31 tells of the highest truth of all revealed to Jeremiah.

The internal evidence of the book of Jeremiah confirms this point. The entire book, with the exception of chapter 31, deals with the "wrath of God." (Chapter 3 is no exception. Chapter 30 may be grouped with chapter 31, but verses 14 and 22 ff. raise doubts on this position.) God's love alone, without any trace of his wrath, is dominant only in chapter 31. (This may reflect the fact that the chapter was written after the catastrophe of God's wrath seen in the destruction of Jerusalem in 586 B.C.) It should be noted that here God's wrath was completely overcome by his love for the first time in Jeremiah's forty years of prophetic activities. What a heartbreaking mission it must have been to proclaim God's wrath for forty years! From this proclamation of wrath, Jeremiah was at last freed. The word of God which Jeremiah heard at this decisive moment was "my bowels are troubled."

God's wrath had passed. (This reminds us of the "Comfort, comfort my people" of Isaiah 40:1.) God's love completely overcame his wrath. Now the people of God would again be received into his love—not only the Southern Kingdom, Judah, but also the Northern Kingdom, Israel. Now God would create something new; Israel, the wife who abandoned her husband Yahweh, will return to him. (This is the meaning of 31:22.)

After the announcement of the "pain of God," we come to the extraordinary proclamation of the "new covenant," verses 31 ff., which is called the "peak of Old Testament religion." There is no question that this "new covenant" plays the most important role not only in Jeremiah 31 but also in the entire Scripture. This "new covenant" seems to presuppose the "pain of God" of verse 20, for the "new covenant" (it may be called the Romans 8 of the Old Testament!) really expresses the "love rooted in the pain of God." Let us now examine this relationship.

Men are capable of turning against God's immediate "love": "not like the covenant which I made with their fathers when I took them by the hand to bring them out of the land of Egypt, my covenant which they broke, though I was their husband" (vs. 32). But they are incapable of turning against God's "pain" which is his love pouring upon those turning against his immediate love: "for I will forgive their iniquity, and I will remember their sin no more" (vs. 34). God completely overcomes men in "his pain": "But this is the covenant which I will make with the house of Israel after those days, says the LORD: I will put my law within them, and I will write it upon their hearts; and I will be their God, and they shall be my people. And no longer shall each man teach his neighbor and each his brother, saying, 'Know the LORD,' for they shall all know me, from the least of them to the greatest" (vss. 33-34). In this sense, God's "pain" is at once his "love": "If the heavens above can be measured, and the foundations of the earth below can be explored, then I will cast off all the descendants of Israel for all that they have done . . . It shall not be uprooted or overthrown any more for ever" (vss. 37, 40).

Thus the internal evidence of the entire book of Jeremiah, the climax of which is the "new covenant," may be summarized in a single expression—"love rooted in the pain of God." It is said that Isaiah saw God's holiness, Hosea saw God's love, and Amos saw God's righteousness. We wish to add that Jeremiah saw God's pain—this "pain" is at once God's "love."

(The significance of Jeremiah's "new covenant" has been seen solely as introducing individuality in religion. But I believe that its primary significance should be seen in the undefeatable love of God in which man cannot break this "new covenant.")

We must finally give attention to one significant point in this exegetical study. The word *hamah*, applied to God, means "pain" and "love" simultaneously. Thus these two meanings are identical and yet different. Being drawn from one word, *hamah*, "pain" and "love" are identical; yet they contain different meanings when viewed from their two different sides. Considered as a unit, "pain" and "love" are one. In this case, "pain" and "love" can be drawn out by analysis. Thus these two concepts coexist side by side in the same locus.

Considered from its two sides, "love" and "pain" are different and one cannot be absorbed by the other. In this case, the element which holds "pain" and "love" together is synthesis. This one element containing "pain" and "love" is to be interpreted both analytically and synthetically.

The structure of grace to which the word refers may be clarified by the above discussion. The victory of God's "pain" is equated with his "love" when his "pain" completely conquers sinners. As love as God's "love" is the victory of his pain, his "love" can be called an extension or echo, an analytical result of his "pain." God's "love" is the other side of his "pain" (Wrede) and both stand on the same locus.

In spite of this fact, "love" is "love" and cannot be absorbed into "pain" because they are different. Therefore a synthesis is required for "pain" and "love" to exist as one. This synthesis is "love rooted in the pain of God." Thus "love rooted in the pain of God" is simultaneously analytic and synthetic.

The relationships between the death and resurrection of Christ and between justification and sanctification constitute the inner structure of grace. The resurrection of Christ as his victory over death inevitably follows his death, since his love conquers all. (See Mark 9:31.) Yet his resurrection is not the same as his death. Sanctification, as his victory, inevitably follows the justification which conquers all disobedience of sinners. Yet sanctification is not the same as justification.

"Love" is the victory of "pain," outside of which there is no real "love." As long as we live in this world, we must recognize the superiority of "pain" over "love." "Love," although present in this world, can never be seen perfectly. The complete victory of God is only his "pain" (justification). "Love" (sanctification) constantly faces defeat. Because of his "pain," God can continually be victor despite the defeat of his "love."

III

Let us reflect on the results of the above exegetical investigations.

1. "Love rooted in the pain of God" concerns the entire message of the Bible, if "love rooted in the pain of God" means that God loves those who reject his love and by conquest makes them obedient to him. For the entire Bible has nothing more than this to say. (This is not a theory, but a proven fact.)

This term, which derives its expression from biblical passages, should not be generalized without careful exegesis, although its message encompasses the entire Bible. The passages in question are Jeremiah 31:20 and Isaiah 63:15. We should never employ an eisegesis as if the entire message of the Bible were condensed in these passages. Only when this term becomes part of the theological vocabulary can it encompass the whole Bible, being liberated from the limitations of a particular passage. The words of the Bible come to possess encompassment only when we move from the realm of exegesis to the realm of systematic theology. "Love rooted in the pain of God" is used as theological terminology because of its extraordinary nature and because of the mystery that "pain" and "love" exist simultaneously.

2. The word "pain," which plays a decisive role in the phrase "love rooted in the pain of God," is symbolic. A "symbol," according to Dr. Seiichi Hatano, "points to that which is suggestive,

breaking away from basic human understanding and remaining outside of this world.[13] Let us recall Calvin's above-cited exposition. According to Calvin, "God attributes human feelings [*humanos affectus*] to himself" and "Such a thing does not properly [*proprie*] belong to God."[14] This is the first characteristic of a symbol. "Pain" certainly is humanly understandable. Yet this word points to "that which is suggestive, breaking away from human understanding and remaining outside of this world"—this is the second and most important characteristic of a symbol. Thus Calvin continues by saying that God "expresses himself imperfectly in terms of human ignorance, knowing no other way to communicate the greatness of his love toward us" (*aliter*).[15]

The above reflections, however, are not sufficient. We find that both of the above two characteristics present many problems. We must admit that real reflection does not end but rather begins at this point.

As to the above *first* point, it is true that words of the Scripture acquire encompassment when used as theological terms, but our intention to create such theological terms must be questioned. Is any selfishness concealed behind our intention? If so, such selfishness is disobedience to the Word of God. But, alas, we cannot even momentarily avoid disobedience to the Word of God. We cannot advance one step without raising the dust of disobedience. Even when we try to witness to the grace of God, our disobedience raises its head. Thus Paul laments over this deepest human contradiction: "Wretched man that I am! Who will deliver me from the body of this death?"

The above *second* point has a problem similar to the first point. Although the words of the Bible may point to divine realities by a symbol of human experiences, our intention of this "pointing" must also be questioned. Here again selfishness may be detected. Calvin says meaningfully, God "expresses himself imperfectly [*crasse*] in terms of human ignorance [*ruditati*]."[16] It is possible that our disobedience may be concealed in this "ignorance." Is it not our guilt that we make God responsible for this "imperfection"? Where do we have the guarantee that this symbol is acceptable to God?

What concerns us here is the problem of sin—sin in reference to theological intentions. Without solving this matter, the preliminary question (*Vorfrage*) of speaking about God cannot be solved. This preliminary question must be answered before each concrete question (*materiale Frage*) concerning the content can be dealt with. Without this, biblical exegesis is impossible, for exegesis is a human act. This preliminary question is one of *prolegomena*, the author's own reflection on his position before he discusses content. Although the content to be discussed may seem to be obedient to the Word of God, does the author's position still reflect his disobedience? This reflection is prolegomena. What is expressed in the prolegomena reveals the author's real intention. Although the discussion of the content may sound "evangelical," the author's legalistic viewpoint becomes his real intention. This is why all intentions must be stated in the prolegomena.

How then will the problem of sin in theological intention be solved? Nothing but the gospel can resolve it. Nothing but the gospel can deliver us. The gospel is also the only solution to the problem of prolegomena. Those who are unable to speak the Word of God without falling into disobedience can no longer be disobedient when they are loved and accepted by God.

Disobedience means separation from God's love, but we can not be separated from God's love which accepts those who are estranged from it. If we cannot be separated from the love of God, then we have become obedient. To remain in the love of God is obedience. When those who cannot pursue theological activity without falling into disobedience are loved and accepted by God, their theological intentions can no longer fall into disobedience. The use of biblical words as theological terms and the use of human experiences as symbols for divine realities are now liberated from disobedience. " . . . thanks be to God . . . through our Lord Jesus Christ"! Thus the problems of the first and second points have been solved. "Love rooted in the pain of God" encompasses the entire Bible, and we have proven "love rooted in the pain of God" boldly and literally. The symbol finds its freedom not in the philosophy of religion, but in the *theology of the cross*.

Here we discover something extraordinary. The phrase "love rooted in the pain of God" becomes an obedient and true witness because of the reality to which it points. The symbol becomes obedient and true because of the reality to which it points. The reality redeems and sustains the symbol. The symbol points to the reality while being redeemed by it. The witness bears witness to the reality while being sustained by it. The content steps out to meet the prolegomena. The gospel steps out to deliver the theologian who proclaims it. This is the basic nature of grace. This is what is meant when it is said that Jesus "loved them to the end" (John 13:1). Grace is all-pervading.

Let us return at this point to Luther's concept of the "hidden God" (*Deus absconditus*) in order to strengthen the above discussion from a different angle. This concept has recently been noted as fundamental to Luther's theology, so much so that Kattenbusch declares that "only those who properly understand this concept of the 'hidden God' can thoroughly understand Luther."[17] Luther used this expression in the sense that God who is the object of our faith works contrary to human reason and concepts. Thus the power of God is hidden (*absconditus*) in weakness, his wisdom in folly, his mercy in severity, his righteousness in sin, and his compassion in wrath.[18] Since God performs his works in a way contrary to human thinking, we can only "believe" and not "see" them. This is the basic nature of faith and we may say that the truth of faith which Luther won at the cost of a lifelong struggle is represented by this short word. Here lies the significance of this concept. Luther came to grasp the important concept *Vere, tu es Deus absconditus* from the Latin version of Isaiah 45:15. He adopted the words of this text and made them encompassing. God came to be described symbolically by these strange words.

Does the original meaning of Isaiah 45:15 justify Luther's interpretation? The opinions of commentators are divided into two groups, depending on whether this verse is interpreted as the words spoken by the Gentiles following verse 14, or spoken by the prophet himself. Such scholars as Ewald, Hitzig, Duhm, Cheyne, Martin, Whitehouse, and others connect the verse with verse 14 and regard it as the words spoken by the Gentiles (the Sabeans) toward the God of Israel. This interpretation, though held by such competent scholars as the above-mentioned ones, merely suggests the "hidden God" unknown to the Gentiles and disagrees completely with Luther's interpretation.

Such scholars as Kittel and Dillman hold the second view and regard the verse as the utterance of the prophet (as does the Japanese Version). Even in this case, the words "hidden God" simply suggest God who performs his great works beyond our comprehension, and such deep meaning as Luther implied cannot be drawn from them alone.

Consequently, Luther's interpretation cannot be justified by the above two views. Does this mean that Luther's "hidden God" conceals selfishness and disobedience both as theological term and as symbol? Here we must consider Luther's position. He was always obedient to faith as a theologian of "faith alone." His theology was confined within this obedience. Those who remember that disobedience was dead in him will not accuse him for this theological term. They would praise the God of grace who by compassion allowed Luther to serve him. The symbol Luther used was redeemed and sustained by the reality to which the words refer. The words "hidden God" were sustained by the grace of God despite their ambiguity.

Yet we must immediately add: "What shall we say then? Are we to continue in sin that grace may abound? By no means! How can we who died to sin still live in it?" (Rom. 6:1-2). We cannot leave the symbol alone in disobedience, though the reality will cause the symbol to die. Those of us who know grace must strive earnestly toward obedience. We must give serious attention to grace in order that it might be recognized not only in our faith, but objectively and scientifically. Frankly, we may say that Luther did not give sufficient effort toward objectifying his concept of the "hidden God." The positivist and the spiritualist are both one-sided. We cannot say therefore that the section on exegetical investigation has been overproportionately detailed.

The reality itself supports the symbol. The support for "love rooted in the pain of God" is found in the reality to which the words point. Thus the words of the symbol and the witness become negative while the reality to which they point becomes positive. The negative aspect is not a theme; it rather serves to draw out the theme itself. The theme means the positive aspect of the symbol and the witness. We can only recognize the reality —grace—when we recognize this positive aspect. The grace of God guarantees that we shall not fall back into disobedience at any given moment and allows us to serve him with joyful freedom. Trust in grace produces simplicity and boldness, born of freedom, and gives positive meaning to the symbol.

Man's pain and God's pain are qualitatively different, "as a dog is different from the Dog Star." (Compare the relation between Christ's cross and our cross, Mark 8:34.) Man's pain is unproductive; it is darkness without light. God's pain is productive; it is darkness with the light of salvation. (This is why God's "pain" is connected with his "love.") But in spite of the difference between these two kinds of pain, they still correspond. Their nature is different, but they have common ground. Standing on this common ground of pain (we are experiencing it now!), we glimpse the image of what is taking place in God's grace. God is in pain. The personification of God's pain is Jesus Christ.

We dare to speak about this "pain of God," for, to use Calvin's words, "God does not express his great love for us in any other way!" We dare to see with Jeremiah God's grace in his "pain." Are not the eyes which saw God's pain frozen? " . . . his appearance was so marred, beyond human semblance, and his form beyond that of the sons of men . . . " (Isa. 52:14). The pain of God is "the wisdom of death" (Overbeck). We cannot behold his pain without risking our life. We must pronounce the words "pain of God" as if we are allowed to speak them only once in our lifetime. Those who have beheld the pain of God cease to be loquacious, and open their mouths only by the passion to bear witness to it.

Those who have seen the pain of God can live without dying, because the "pain" is at once "love." By this "love," man's pain is purified and becomes like God's "pain."

"Love rooted in the pain of God" cannot be observed objectively outside of our human experience. There is no way to see it other than experiencing it in our own life.

I am therefore closing this chapter with such a subjective description, though I advocated the need for an objective study at the beginning.

NOTES

Abbreviations

W. A. Martin Luther, *Sämtliche Werke* (Weimar: Böhlau, *Weimarer Ausgabe*, 1883).

E. A. Martin Luther, *Lutheri Opera* (Erlangen: Karl Hender, *Erlangen Ausgabe*, 1934).

CHAPTER ONE: GOD IN PAIN

1. Luther, W. A., Vol. 40, Part 1, p. 273.
2. Theodosius Harnack, *Luthers Theologie* (München: Christoph Kaiser, 1927), *Neue Ausgabe*, Vol. 1, p. 338.
3. Luther, *op. cit.*, Vol. 45, p. 370.
4. Luther, E. A., Vol. 24, p. 422.
5. Masahisa Uemura, *Uemura Zenshu* (*Uemura's Complete Works*) (Tokyo: Kankokai, 1932), Vol. 4, p. 331.
6. Martin Luther, *Lectures on Romans*, ed. and tr. by Wilhelm Pauck (Philadelphia: The Westminster Press, 1961), Library of Christian Classics, pp. 179-180.
7. Karl Barth, *Die Theologie und die Kirche* (Zürich: Evangelischer Verlag, n.d.), pp. 190 ff.
8. *Ibid.*, p. 200.
9. *Ibid.*, p. 190.
10. *Ibid.*, p. 211.
11. Karl Barth, *The Epistle to the Romans*, tr. from the 6th edition by Edwyn C. Hoskyns (London: Oxford University Press, 1933), p. 39.
12. Karl Barth, *Credo* (New York: Charles Scribner's Sons, 1962), p. 14.
13. *Ibid.*, p. 18.
14. Karl Barth, *Gottes Wille und unsere Wünsche* (*Theologische Existenz Heute*, Heft 7) (München: Kaiser, 1934), p. 6.
15. Emil Brunner, *The Mediator*, tr. by Olive Wyon (Philadelphia: The Westminster Press, 1957).
16. Karl Barth, *Church Dogmatics* (Edinburgh: T. & T. Clark, 1957), Vol. II, Part 1, p. 612.

Translator's note: The English translation quoted reads "rift" instead of "pain." The latter word is chosen as being closer to the German *Schmerzen* and the sense taken by Dr. Kitamori.

17. Albrecht Ritschl, *Rechtfertigung und Versöhonung*, 3rd ed. (Bonn: A. Marcus und E. Webers Verlag, 1903), Vol. III, p. 260.

18. Friedrich Daniel Ernst Schleiermacher, *Reden über Religion*, 4th Revised Edition (Göttingen: Vandenhoeck und Ruprecht, 1920), pp. 32 and 164.

19. Friedrich Schleiermacher, *The Christian Faith*, ed. by H. B. Mackintosh and J. S. Stewart (Edinburgh: T. & T. Clark, 1928), §100, 3; §101, 4.

20. Johannes Wendland, *Die religiöse Entwicklung Schleiermachers* (Tübingen: J. C. B. Mohr, 1915), p. 181.

21. *Ibid.*, p. 309.

22. Wilhelm Herrmann, *Der Verkehr des Christen mit Gott* (Tübingen: J. C. B. Mohr, 1921), p. 75.

23. Adolph Harnack, *What Is Christianity?*, tr. by Thomas Bailey Saunders (New York: G. P. Putnam's Sons, 1901), p. 154.

24. Friedrich Wilhelm Joseph von Schelling, *Philosophische Untersuchungen über das Wesen der Menschlichen Freiheit* (Leipzig: Felix Meiner, 1809), p. 55. (Page reference is to Japanese translation by K. Nishitani.)

25. *Ibid.*, pp. 158-159, and 151, 157, of Japanese translation.

26. *Ibid.*, p. 147 of Japanese translation.

27. *Ibid.*, p. 84 of Japanese translation.

28. Daiei Kaneko, *Nippon Bukkyo Shikan* (A History of Japanese Buddhism) (Tokyo: Iwanami Shoten, 1940), p. 147.
    Translator's note: Shotoku Taishi (A.D. 572-622) is a famous name in Japanese history. Second son of the Emperor Yomei and for some years regent, he is popularly credited with being influential in introducing Buddhism to Japan. The *Yuimakyo* are Buddhist scriptures.

29. *Ibid.*, p. 147.

30. *Ibid.*, p. 149.

31. Hajime Tanabe, *Jitsuzon Gainen no Hatten* (The Development of the Existential Concept) (*Tetsugaku Kenkyu*) (Philosophical Studies), No. 309, pp. 10-11.
    Translator's note: Dr. Tanabe (1885-1962) bears one of the most distinguished names in modern Japanese philosophy. He joined the faculty of philosophy at Kyoto University in 1920 where he remained till his retirement. His chief field of study was the German idealistic philosophy. His many volumes show a strong Christian influence.

32. Hajime Tanabe, *Hegel Tetsugaku to Benshoho* (Hegel's Philosophy and Dialectic) (Tokyo: Iwanami Shoten), p. 53.

33. Norinaga Motoori, *Kojikiden* (Commentary on the Kojiki), Section 27.
    Translator's note: Motoori (1730-1801) was one of the three great scholars whose studies in Japanese literature and history stimulated the Shinto revival and contributed to the restoration of the Emperor in 1868. His principal work was a commentary in 44 volumes on the *Kojiki*, the first written Japanese history, cosmogony, and mythology. The quotation is taken from this commentary. Prince Yamato Takeru (*circa* 81-113) was the third son of the Emperor Keiko.

CHAPTER TWO: THE PAIN OF GOD AND THE HISTORICAL JESUS

1. William Wrede, *Paulus,* 2nd ed.
2. *Ibid.,* p. 86.
3. *Ibid.,* p. 87.
4. *Ibid.,* p. 94.
5. *Ibid.,* p. 95.
6. *Ibid.,* p. 84.
7. *Ibid.,* p. 106.
8. Ernst Ludwig Enders, *Martin Luthers Briefwechsel* (Calwer & Stuttgart: Verlag der Vereins-buchhandlung, 1889), Band 3, p. 208.
9. Wrede, *op. cit.,* p. 103.
10. *Ibid.,* p. 95.
11. *Ibid.,* p. 105.
12. Kazoh Kitamori, *Jujika no Shu (Lord of the Cross)* (Tokyo: Shinseido, 1940), pp. 43-46.
13. Edwin Abbott Abbott, cited in James Moffatt, *The Theology of the Gospels* (London: Duckworth & Co., 1912), p. 94.
14. Alfred Ernest Garvie, *The Christian Ideal for Human Society* (London: Hodder & Stoughton, 1930), p. 155.
15. Heinrich Denifle, *Luther in rationalistischer und christlicher Beleuchtung* (Mainz: Verlag von Kirchheim, 1904), p. 34.
16. P. T. Forsyth, *The Person and Place of Jesus Christ* (London: Independent Press, Ltd., 1909), p. 168.
17. *Ibid.,* p. 266.
18. Moffatt, *op. cit.,* pp. 54-55, 58, 69.
19. Forsyth, *op. cit.,* p. 271.
20. Luther, W. A., Vol. 36, p. 180.

CHAPTER THREE: PAIN AS THE ESSENCE OF GOD

1. Uemura, *op. cit.,* Vol. 3, p. 403.
2. Forsyth, *op. cit.,* p. 270.
3. Theodosius Harnack, *op. cit.,* Vol. 2, pp. 242-243.
4. *Ibid.,* p. 253.
5. Luther, W. A., Vol. 45, p. 415; Theodosius Harnack, p. 76.
6. Luther, E. A., Vol. 12, p. 324; Vol. 9, p. 381; Theodosius Harnack, p. 84.
7. Luther, W. A., Vol. 50, p. 274.
8. Francis J. Hall, *Dogmatic Theology* (New York: Longmans Green & Co., 1923), Vol. 4, pp. 267-268.
9. Augustine, *De Trinitate,* Vol. 5, 15, 228.

CHAPTER FOUR: SERVICE FOR THE PAIN OF GOD

1. Luther, E. A., el. 18, 267.
2. Barth, *Church Dogmatics*, Vol. I (1955), §1, p. x.

CHAPTER FIVE: THE SYMBOL OF THE PAIN OF GOD

1. Theodosius Harnack, *op. cit.*, Vol. 2, p. 338.
2. Adam C. Welch, *Visions of the End: A Study in Daniel and Revelation* (London: James Clarke, 1922), p. 198.
3. John Calvin, *Commentary on Jeremiah, Corpus Reformatorum*, tr. by John Owen (Grand Rapids: Wm. B. Eerdmans, 1950), p. 109.
4. Andrew Bruce Davidson, *Old Testament Prophecy* (Edinburgh: T. & T. Clark, 1904), pp. 240 ff.
5. Quoted from the Japanese translation (Jiro Kojima, *Shukyo Shisohen*, pp. 254-255) of Dmitri Sergeievich Merezhkovsky, *Tolstoi and Dostoevski.*
6. Kiyoshi Miki, *Pascal ni okeru Ningen no Kenkyu* (*The Study of Man in Pascal*) (Tokyo: Iwanami Shoten, 1928), p. 220.
7. Blaise Pascal, *The Thoughts of Blaise Pascal*, tr. by C. Kegan Paul (London: Regan Paul, Trench & Co., 1880), p. 231.
8. Takashi Ide, *Kami no Omoi* (*The Thought of God*) (Tokyo: Ohmura Shoten, 1924), p. 204.
9. John Skinner, *Isaiah* (Cambridge: Cambridge University Press, 1917), Vol. II, p. 270.
10. Davidson, *op. cit.*, p. 464.
11. Skinner, *op. cit.*, Vol. II, p. 279.
12. Arthur Samuel Peake, *The Servant of Yahweh* (Manchester: Manchester University Press, 1931), pp. 8-9.
13. Davidson, *op. cit.*, pp. 466-467. George Adam Smith, *The Book of Isaiah* (New York: Harper & Brothers Publishers, 1927), Vol. I, pp. 57 ff.
14. Henry Wheeler Robinson, *The Cross of the Servant* (London: Student Christian Movement, 1926), pp. 42-43.
15. *Ibid.* (No page reference.)
16. G. W. Wade, *The Book of the Prophet Isaiah*, p. lxvi.
17. Robinson, *op. cit.*, p. 64.
18. Arthur S. Peake, *The Problem of Suffering in the Old Testament* (London: Epworth Press, 1947), p. 191; Peake, *The Servant of Yahweh*, pp. 65 ff.
19. Peake, *The Servant of Yahweh*, p. 63.
20. Henry Wheeler Robinson, *The Religious Ideas of the Old Testament* (London: Duckworth & Co., 1913), pp. 203-204; Skinner, *op. cit.*, pp. 36 ff.; Alexander Francis Kirkpatrick, *The Doctrine of the Prophets* (London: Macmillan, 1901), pp. 389-390, 393.

21. Smith, *op. cit.*, pp. 261, 266, 275-276; Robinson, *The Religious Ideas of the Old Testament*, pp. 36, 83; Skinner, *op. cit.*, Vol. II, pp. 36-37, 279; Wade, *op. cit.*, pp. lxv-lxvi.
22. Plachte, *Symbol und Idol*, p. 110.
23. Skinner, *op. cit.*, pp. 279-280; Robinson, *The Religious Ideas of the Old Testament*, p. 36; Peake, *The Servant of Yahweh*, p. 73.
24. Max Haller, *Die Schriften des Alten Testaments* (Tübingen: J. C. B. Mohr, 1940), Vol. 3, p. 67; Charles Culter Torrey, *The Second Isaiah* (Edinburgh: T. & T. Clark, 1928), p. 147.
25. John Skinner, *Prophecy and Religion* (Cambridge: Cambridge University Press, 1951), p. 229.
26. Davidson, *op. cit.*, p. 459.
27. Peake, *The Problem of Suffering in the Old Testament*, p. 88; Peake, *The Servant of Yahweh*, pp. 62-63.
28. Robinson, *The Religious Ideas of the Old Testament*, p. 76.
29. Wade, *op. cit.*, p. lxvi.
30. Robinson, *The Religious Ideas of the Old Testament*, p. 76.
31. Smith, *op. cit.*, Vol. II, pp. 288-289.
32. K. Kohler, *Jewish Theology*, p. 376.
33. Smith, *op. cit.*, Vol. II, p. 318.
34. *Ibid.*, pp. 359-360, 362-363.
35. *Ibid.*, p. 363.
36. *Ibid.*, pp. 355-356 and 351.
37. Translator's note: From the *Manyoshu* (*The Myriad Leaves*), an anthology of more than four thousand poems, covering three hundred years, compiled by A.D. 760.
38. H. Preserved Smith, *O. T. History*, p. 290.
39. John Merlin Powis Smith, *The Prophets and Their Times*, 2nd ed. (Chicago: University of Chicago Press, 1941), pp. 239-240.

CHAPTER SIX: THE MYSTICISM OF PAIN

1. Luther, W. A., Vol. 1, p. 336.
2. Martin Luther, *Luthers Vorlesung über den Römerbrief*, ed. by Johannes Ficker (Leipzig: Dieterich'sche Verlagshandlung, 1925), Vol. 1, p. 54.
3. Shogo Yamaya, *Roma-sho* (*Epistle to the Romans*) (Tokyo: Shinkyo Shuppansha, 1952), p. 157.
4. Rudolf Otto, *Aufsätze das Numinose betreffend*, 4th ed. (Gotha: Leopold Klotz, 1929), p. 82.
5. Shogo Yamaya, *Paul no Shingaku* (*The Theology of Paul*) (Tokyo: Nagasaki Shoten, 1936), pp. 172-177; quotation from p. 177.
6. Otto, *op. cit.*, pp. 82-83.
7. Luther, *Lectures on Romans*, Vol. 15, p. 182.
8. *Ibid.*, p. 222.
9. Otto, *op. cit.*, pp. 82-83.

10. Luther, W. A., Vol. 1, p. 137, and Vol. 37, p. 410.
11. Johannes Schneider, *Die Passionsmystik des Paulus* (Leipzig: J. C. Hinrichs, 1929), p. 168.
12. Augustine, *Contra Julianum*, II, 9, 32.
13. Pascal, *op. cit.*, p. 233.
14. Emile Boutroux, *Pascal* (Paris: Librairie Hachette et Cie., 1907), pp. 26-27.
15. *Ibid.*, p. 189.
16. *Ibid.*, p. 144.
17. *Ibid.*, p. 145.
18. *Ibid.*

CHAPTER SEVEN: THE PAIN OF GOD AND ETHICS

1. Luther, *Lectures on Romans*, p. 263.
2. *Ibid.*, p. 260.
3. Takeo Ito, *Hidarite no Sho* (*Left-handed Writing*) (Tokyo: Banrikaku, 1940), p. 91. Author's italics.
4. Augsburg Confession, Article 2, tr. from the *Book of Concord*, ed. by Theodore G. Tappert (Philadelphia: Muhlenberg Press, 1959), p. 29.
5. Augustine, *De Trinitate*, V, 10. Translated here from the Japanese.
6. Translator's note: "Emotion" here is a translation of *joh*, which actually has a wider meaning than "emotion." *Kanjo* is closest to the English "emotion." "Emotion and feeling" would be closer to what is implied by *joh*.
7. Luther, *Lectures on Romans*, pp. 255 and 260.
8. Karl Adam, *Das Wesen des Katholozismus*, p. 225 of the Japanese translation.
9. On Matthew 9:13: See Meyer, pp. 197 ff.; A. Carr, p. 83; A. H. McNeile, p. 120; Plummer, p. 140.
   On Mark 2:17: See Gould, p. 43; A. E. J. Rawlinson, pp. 29 f.
   On Luke 5:31-32: See Farrer, pp. 121 f.; Adeney, p. 113; Creed, p. 82; Plummer, p. 161.
   On Luke 15:7: See Meyer, pp. 450 f.; Plummer, p. 319; Manson, p. 177; Godet, II, pp. 144 ff.
   On Luke 18:9-14: See Plummer, p. 420; Manson, p. 202.
10. Kanzo Uchimura, *Uchimura Zenshu* (*Uchimura's Complete Works*) (Tokyo: Iwanami Shoten, 1933), Vol. 12, p. 436.
11. *Ibid.*, p. 191.
12. *Ibid.*, Vol. 20, p. 24.
13. Enders, *op. cit.*, p. 208.
14. Anders Nygren, *Agape and Eros* (Philadelphia: The Westminster Press, 1953), p. 52.
15. *Ibid.*, p. 75.
16. *Ibid.*, p. 123.

17. William Adams Brown, *Christian Theology in Outline* (Edinburgh: T. & T. Clark, 1931), p. 100.
18. Nygren, *op. cit.*, p. 118.
19. Brown, *op. cit.*, p. 88.
20. Erich Seeberg, *Luthers Theologie—Motive und Ideen*, Vol. 1: *Die Gottesanschauung* (Göttingen: Vandenhoeck und Ruprecht, 1929), pp. 131-132.
21. Luther, *Lectures on Romans*, p. 327.
22. Karl Holl, *Augustins innere Entwicklung* in *Gesammelte Aufsätze*, Vol. 3 (Tübingen: J. C. B. Mohr, 1929), p. 87.
23. *Ibid.*, p. 109.
24. *Ibid.*, Vol. 1, p. 165.
25. *Ibid.*, p. 179.

CHAPTER EIGHT: THE IMMANENCE AND
TRANSCENDENCE OF THE PAIN OF GOD

1. Luther, W. A., Vol. 40, 1, 241; Martin Luther, *Lectures on Galatians*, tr. by Jaroslav Pelikan, in *Luther's Works*, American Edition, Vol. 26 (St. Louis: Concordia Publishing House, 1963), p. 138.
   Translator's note: In a footnote, Pelikan writes: "For the Latin *solarii*, used by Luther's detractors, we have borrowed the Wesleyan term, 'solafideists.' "

CHAPTER NINE: THE PAIN OF GOD AND
THE HIDDEN GOD

1. For an exegetical study of this, see the appendix.
2. Luther, W. A., Vol. 18, p. 481.
3. *Ibid.*, p. 663.
4. Luther, *Lectures on Romans*, p. 264.
5. *Ibid.*, p. 246.
6. *Ibid.*, p. 242.
7. Seeberg, *op. cit.*, pp. 60-61.
8. *Ibid.*, p. 96.
9. Ferdinand Kattenbusch, *Die deutsche evangelische Theologie seit Schleiermacher* (Giessen: Alfred Topelmann Verlag, 1934), p. 151.
10. Seeberg, *op. cit.*, p. 98.
11. *Ibid.*, p. 142.
12. Luther, *Lectures on Romans*, p. 262.
13. Paul Althaus, *Theologische Aufsätze* (Gütersloh: C. Bertelsmann Verlag, 1929), Vol. 1, p. 114.
14. Luther, W. A., Vol. 1, pp. 557-558.
15. Luther, *Lectures on Romans*, p. 242. Cf. pp. 263-264.
16. The passage quoted in the author's *Shingaku to Shinjo* (*Theology and*

Creed), p. 23, is typical of Luther's thought along these lines. Theodosius Harnack praised this side of his thought.

17. Althaus, *op. cit.*, Vol. 1, p. 10.
18. *Ibid.*, p. 11.
19. Luther, W. A., Vol. 7, p. 548.
20. *Ibid.*, Vol. 18, p. 663.
21. From *The Lutheran* (June 1936), published by the former Japan Lutheran Church, and the *Karyokai Bulletin* of the YMCA in the former Fifth Higher School, Kumamoto.
22. Luther, *Lectures on Romans*, pp. 262-263.
23. *Ibid.*, p. 330.
24. John Baillie, *The Place of Jesus Christ in Modern Christianity* (Edinburgh: T. & T. Clark, 1929), p. 45.
25. My translation. See original.
      Translator's note: The Greek permits two translations. Dr. Kitamori has selected one which the King James Version gives—used in the text —with J. B. Phillips and C. K. Williams. Other authorities and translations prefer the rendering followed by the Revised Standard Version: "every one whose name has not been written before the foundation of the world in the book of life of the Lamb that was slain."
26. John Calvin, *Christianae Religio Institutio*, III, 9, 1.

CHAPTER TEN: THE ORDER OF LOVE

1. Dante Alighieri, *The Divine Comedy, Inferno*, tr. by John Ciardi, The New American Library of World Literature (New York: Mentor Books, 1954), p. 42.
2. *Ibid.*, p. 43.
3. P. T. Forsyth, *The Justification of God* (London: Independent Press Ltd, 1917), p. 146.
4. Luther, W. A., Vol. 36, p. 435.
5. *Deine Wunden sollen werden*
   Meine Wohnstatt auf der Erden.
                              Johann Scheffler

CHAPTER ELEVEN: THE PAIN OF GOD AND GOSPEL HISTORY

1. Concerning the concept of gospel history, see the author's *Shingaku to Shinjo* (*Theology and Creed*), pp. 28 ff.
2. Calvin, *Institutio*, I, 11, 13.
3. Reinhold Seeberg, *Lehrbuch der Dogmengeschichte* (Leipzig: A. Deichertoche Verlagsbuchhandlung, 1917), Vol. 4, p. 7.
4. Luther, *Tischreden*, W. A., Vol. 2, 1928.

5. Melanchthon, *Corpus Reformatorum*, Vol. 21, p. 837; Vol. 24, p. 309; Vol. 25, pp. 862 ff.
6. For the relation between creed and theology, see the author's *Shingaku to Shinjo*, pp. 77 ff.
7. Translator's note: The author explained "monism of light" to the translator as follows. Japanese thinking tries to avoid thoughts about death. Rather, by looking on the bright side of things, it tries to be positive and not negative.

   In the translator's opinion this can hardly be called a "monism of light." However, he has let the phrase stand as being a literal translation from the Japanese, and in accordance with the author's wish.
8. Translator's note: Matsuomaru is a retainer who has taken new service after the exile of his former feudal lord. The enemies of the latter are seeking his heir, and narrow the search to a *terakoya*, a school for boys housed in a Buddhist temple. Matsuomaru knows that the only way to save the heir's life is to substitute his own son, and sends him to the temple school. Genzo, also a former retainer of the exiled lord, runs the school. Bound by the same ties of loyalty as Matsuomaru, he becomes party to the deception. The heir's life is saved at the cost of the life of Matsuomaru's son.

   The four Japanese tragedies named in the pages of this chapter are *kabuki*, the classical drama of Japan. In each of them a life is sacrificed, usually a son by his parents, to save someone whose claims to this type of devotion seemed paramount. If this seems barbarous, remember the story of Abraham and Isaac; surely God's revelation to Abraham acquires increased significance in the light of what is narrated here. The poignancy of the Japanese tragedy, of course, lies in the conflict between parental love and sacred obligation.
9. Translator's note: The sense of *tsurasa* is best expressed by the Latin phrase *lacrimae rerum*. It is the feeling of inevitable fate and sorrow that overhangs human life. Star-crossed lovers, parting never to meet again, feel the *tsurasa* in their destiny.
10. See Note 8 above.
11. Translator's note: The Japanese saying used to be, "The span of life is fifty years."

CHAPTER TWELVE: THE PAIN OF GOD
AND ESCHATOLOGY

1. Luther, Letter to his father, November 21, 1521.
2. Luther, *Tischreden*, W. A., Vol. 1, 108, #258.
3. Paul Althaus, *Die letzten Dinge*, 4th ed. (Gütersloh: C. Bertelsmann, 1933), pp. 48-51; *Theologische Aufsätze*, Vol. 1, pp. 117-118.

CHAPTER THIRTEEN: CONCLUSION

1. Paul Valéry.
2. Shiro Hibino, "Yasen Byoin" ("The Field Hospital"), a short story in *Gosho Kuriku* (*Gosho Creek*) (Tokyo: Chuo Koronsha, 1939).
3. Translator's note: Hidesaburo Saito's dictionary defines *yoyuh* as: "reserve, something to spare; a margin." Thus it is much wider than what is meant by "leisure" and is applied to money, energy, etc. There is no one word in English by which it can be rendered.

APPENDIX

1. See Gesenius, *Hebräisches und aramäisches Handwörterbach über d. A. T.*, p. 184; David Cassel, *Hebräisch-deutsches Wörterbuch*, 10 Auflage, p. 79.
2. John Calvin, *Commentary on Jeremiah* (Edinburgh: The Calvin Translation Society, 1854), Vol. 2, pp. 106-109.
3. C. F. Keil, *Biblischer Kommentar über die Prophet Jeremia* (1872), p. 329.
4. Arthur Samuel Peake, *Jeremiah* (Edinburgh: T. C. & E. C. Jack, 1911), Vol. 2, p. 94.
5. F. Löhr Giesebrecht, *Jeremia, Handkommentar zum Alten Testament* (Göttingen: Vandenhoeck, 1907), p. 160.
6. Peake, *Jeremiah*, Vol. 1, p. 30.
7. Wrede, *Paulus*, p. 61. He calls this other side of one piece *Kehrseite* (the reverse).
8. C. R. 36, 309.
9. *Jesaia*, p. 224.
10. C. R. 31, 542.
11. *I. C. C. Psalms*, Vol. 2, p. 25.
12. C. R. 31, 712.
13. Seiichi Hatano, *Shukyo Tetsugaku* (*The Philosophy of Religion*) (Tokyo: Iwanami Shoten, 1935), p. 47.
14. C. R. 38, 677.
15. *Ibid.*
16. *Ibid.*
17. Kattenbusch, *op. cit.*, p. 151.
18. Luther, *Römerbrief*, II, pp. 204, 208, 219; W. A., 18, p. 663, etc.

INDEX OF NAMES

Abbott, Edwin Abbott, 37-38, 171
Adam, Karl, 91, 174
Adeney, W. F., 174
Althaus, Paul, 108, 109-110, 144, 175, 176, 177
Anselm, 34
Arnold, Matthew, 65
Athanasius, 15, 59, 131, 132
Augustine, 35, 48-49, 75, 78, 87, 96-97, 117, 130, 171, 174

Baillie, John, 115, 176
Barth, Karl, 22-23, 55, 106, 169, 172
Bernard of Clairvaux, 78, 130
Boutroux, Emile, 79-80, 81, 174
Briggs, C. A., 158
Brown, William Adams, 92-93, 175
Brunner, Emil, 11, 23, 74, 169

Calvin, John, 16, 60, 116, 130, 153, 154, 155, 158, 163, 167, 172, 176, 178
Carr, A., 174
Cassel, David, 152, 178
Cheyne, T. K., 165
Creed, J. M., 174

Dante, 119, 176
Davidson, Andrew Bruce, 60, 65, 67, 172, 173
Delitzsch, F., 65, 158, 159
Denifle, Heinrich, 38, 171
Dillman, A., 166
Dostoevsky, Feodor, 60, 172
Duhm, B., 165

Enders, Ernst, 35, 92, 171, 174
Ewald, H., 165

Farrer, F. W., 174
Feuerbach, L., 153

Forsyth, P. T., 40, 43, 45, 59, 120, 171, 176

Garvie, Alfred Ernest, 38, 171
Genzo, 176
Gesenius, W., 152, 153, 178
Giesebrecht, F. Löhr, 155
Godet, F., 174
Gould, E. F., 174

Hall, Francis J., 48, 171
Haller, Max, 66, 173
Harnack, Adolph, 24, 35, 38, 130, 170
Harnack, Theodosius, 21, 45, 58, 169, 171, 172, 176
Hatano, Seiichi, 162-163, 178
Hegel, Georg, 27-30, 170
Herrmann, Wilhelm, 24, 170
Hibino, Shiro, 148, 178
Hilary, 89
Hilty, C., 73
Hitzig, 165
Holl, Karl, 82, 95, 96, 97, 175

Ide, Takashi, 64-65, 172
Ignatius, 115
Ito, Takeo, 86, 174

Kagawa, Toyohiko, 7
Kan, Shusai, 138
Kaneko, Daiei, 26, 27, 170
Kant, Immanuel, 30, 89, 96, 97, 149, 157
Kattenbusch, Ferdinand, 106, 112, 165, 175, 178
Kautzsch, E., 158
Keiko (Emperor), 170
Keil, C. F., 155, 158, 178
Kierkegaard, Søren, 15, 19, 24, 51, 85, 115
Kirkpatrick, Alexander, 66, 172

Kitamori, Kazoh, 12, 15, 36, 169, 171, 175-176, 177
Kittel, R., 19, 166
Kohler, K., 68, 173

Luther, Martin, 8, 15, 16, 21, 22, 35, 39, 43, 45-46, 48, 52, 71, 76, 77, 78, 83, 85, 86, 88-89, 92, 95-96, 97, 102, 105-109, 110-111, 112, 113-114, 123, 130, 133, 141-142, 153-154, 158, 165, 166, 169, 171, 172, 173, 174, 175, 176, 177, 178

McNeile, A. H., 174
Manson, 174
Martin, K., 165
Matsuomaru, 134, 177
Melanchthon, 130, 177
Menge, H., 155
Merezhkovsky, Dmitri Sergeievich, 60, 172
Meyer, H. A. W., 174
Michalson, Carl, 7
Miki, Kiyoshi, 62, 172
Mo, Ti, 86, 88
Moffatt, James, 37-38, 41, 171
Motoori, Norinaga, 31, 170
Myers, F. W. H., 66

Nietzsche, Friedrich, 153
Nygren, Anders, 92-93, 95, 174, 175

Orelli, C., 159
Otto, Rudolf, 59, 72, 75, 76, 173
Overbeck, 167

Pascal, Blaise, 64, 79, 80, 117, 172, 174
Peake, Arthur, 65, 66, 67, 155-156, 158, 159, 172, 173, 178
Pelagius, 78
Pelikan, Jaroslav, 175
Périer, Gilberte, 80
Phillips, J. B., 176
Plachte, 66, 173
Plato, 102
Plummer, A., 174

Rawlinson, A. E. J., 174

Ritschl, Albrecht, 23-24, 170
Robinson, Henry Wheeler, 66, 67, 172, 173

Saito, Hidesaburo, 178
Scheffler, Johann, 124, 176
Schelling, Friedrich, 25-26, 170
Schleiermacher, Friedrich, 24, 170
Schneider, Johannes, 77, 174
Seeberg, Erich, 95-96, 106, 107, 130, 175, 176
Shakespeare, William, 135
Shotoku, Taishi (Prince), 26, 170
Skinner, John, 65, 66, 67, 172, 173
Smith, George Adam, 66, 67-68, 69, 172, 173
Smith, H. Preserved, 70, 173
Smith, J. M. Powis, 70, 173
Staerk, W., 158

Taira, Atsumori, 138
Taira, Koremori, 138
Tanabe, Hajime, 30, 170
Tauler, J., 106, 130
Tolstoy, Leo, 60, 172
Torrey, Charles, 66, 173

Uchimura, Kanzo, 7, 91-92, 174
Uemura, Masahisa, 21-22, 44, 169, 171

Valéry, Paul, 147, 178

Wade, G. W., 66, 67, 172, 173
Welch, Adam C., 59, 172
Wendland, Johannes, 24, 170
Wessel, J., 130
Whitehouse, O. C., 165
Williams, C. K., 176
Wrede, William, 33-34, 36, 38, 156, 161, 171, 178

Yamato, Takeru (Prince), 31, 170
Yamaya, Shogo, 72, 75, 173
Yomei (Emperor), 170
Yoshimura, Sadaji, 135

Zinzendorf, N. L., 77

INDEX OF SCRIPTURE PASSAGES

GENESIS
12 51
15-18 51
22 51
22:1 51
22:2 51
22:12 51
22:12-13 51
22:18 51

EXODUS
33:20 145
33:22 145
33:23 146

JOB
12:6 63
21:7-13 63
21:23-24 63

PSALMS
23:4 124
38:8 .... 152, 158
39:6 152
42:5 152
42:11 152
43:5 152
46:6 151
55:17 .... 16, 152, 158
59:6 151
63:5-8 124
77:3 ..... 16, 152, 158
81:7 106
94:18 149
119:67 147

SONG OF SOLOMON
5:4 .... 152, 158

ISAIAH
1:13 21
16:11 ...... 152, 158

17:12 151
40:1 160
42:1-4 .... 65, 69
42:3 69
42:18-21 66
42:24 66
42:25 66
45:14 165
45:15 ...... 105, 165
49:1-6 65
49:3 .... 65, 68
49:6 69
50:4-9 65
50:5 66
52:10-13 69
52:11 66
52:13 ...... 66, 69
52:13–53:12 65
52:14 167
53:5 22
53:7-9 69
59:11 151
63:9 59
63:15 ..... 9, 21, 64,
    121, 123, 143, 151-
    152, 156-157, 159, 162
63:16 ... 121, 123, 157

JEREMIAH
2:12 44
3 159
3:20 91
4:19 .... 152, 157, 158
4:19-20 61
4:26 61
5:22 151
11:20 67
12:3 67
13:21-22 61
15:6 21
15:17-18 67

18:21-23 67
20:8 64
30 159
30:14 159
30:22 ff. 159
31 .... 159, 160
31:15-22 159
31:20 8,
    9, 16, 19, 21, 44,
    59, 60, 119, 121, 151-
    154, 155-159, 160, 162
31:22 160
31:31 ff. 160
31:32 160
31:33-34 160
31:34 160
31:37 160
31:40 160
40:1 159
48:36 ...... 16, 152

LAMENTATIONS
1:5 61
1:12 61
2:13 64

EZEKIEL
5:13 21

HOSEA
2:20 .... 93, 123
4:17 118
5:15 147
6:1 119
10:2 118
11:1 118
11:2 118
11:4 118
11:8 119
14:4 119

MATTHEW

3:17 118
5:14 90
5:17 38
5:45 38
6:25 ff. 38, 39
9:1-8 103
9:13 ..... 37, 91, 174
10:28-31 124
10:37 54
10:38 .... 50, 54
13:44 102
13:46 102
16:21-23 37
16:22 ...... 24-25, 159
16:24 50
16:25 52
17:9-13 37
17:22 37
20:28 37
22:37-40 99
22:39 99
24 139
24:3 139
24:8 139
24:14 139
24:21 .... 140, 142
24:28 141
24:36 141
25 .... 100, 101
25:16 19
25:18 19
25:31-46 98
25:40 .... 98, 103
25:45 99
26:6-9 100
26:6-13 .... 37, 98
26:9 102
26:10-11 100
26:11 102
26:12 100
26:13 101
26:24 37
26:26-29 37
26:42 37
26:54 37

MARK

1:32-34 40-41

2:1-12 41
2:17 ...... 37, 91, 174
8:31-33 37
8:34 167
9:9-13 37
9:12 ...... 24, 37, 127
9:31 162
10:45 37
12:28 99
13:19 140
13:24 142
13:26 142
14:3-9 37
14:21 37
14:22-25 37

LUKE

2:35 56
5:31 37
5:31-32 174
5:32 91
6:27-28 93
6:32-34 93
6:35 93
6:36 93
7:41-50 37
9:22 37
9:44 37
12:4 .... 124, 125
12:4-5 ...... 124, 127
12:4-7 124-126
12:5 .... 124, 125
12:6 124
12:6-7 ...... 124, 127
12:7 .... 124, 125
13:6-9 37
14:26 .... 75, 84
14:27 113
15 155
15:1-32 37
15:7 174
15:11 ff. 118
15:20 122
15:28 ff. 119
16:19 63
16:19 ff. 63
16:23 63
16:25 63
17:20 139

17:25 .... 141, 142
18:9-14 ...... 37, 174
19:1-10 37
21:22 142
21:23 142
21:25 141
21:28 141
21:29-31 141
21:34 142
21:36 142
22:15-20 37
22:22 37
23:34 37
23:39-43 37

JOHN

1:14 43
3:16 43
3:35 118
5:17-18 42
5:20 118
7:29-30 42
8:58-59 42
10:17 118
10:30-33 42
12:25 .... 75, 76
13:1 165
14:26 40
15:9-10 118
15:12 90
15:26 40
16:7 40
16:13 40
16:23 140
17:23-26 118
19:7 42

ACTS

17:26-27 128
20:28 94

ROMANS

1:17 58
1:24 118
1:26 118
3:21 58
3:31 38-39
4:18 20

Romans (*continued*)

5 155
5:1 111
5:3 .... 110, 111
5:7-8 138
5:8 91
5:10 .... 91, 92
6:1-2 166
6:3 115
6:3-4 71
6:4 72
6:5 .... 71, 72
6:6 .... 71, 72
6:7 77
6:8 .... 71, 72
6:23 .... 52, 113
7:24 163
8 .... 39, 160
8:3 .... 32, 34
8:13 84
8:24-25 123
8:29 121
9:2 .... 86, 103
10:2 140
11:11 128
11:11-12 128-129
11:15 128
11:25 128
11:32 110-111
12:15 85
15:30 72

I CORINTHIANS

1:18 .... 21, 119
1:21 119
1:23 .... 114, 119
1:25 119
2:2 .... 47, 123
2:10 19
4:13 150
7:26 140

12:3 114
13 39
13:12 146
15 39
16:24 88

II CORINTHIANS

1:5 .... 71, 72, 75
3:18 .... 72, 146
4:10 64
5:16 32
5:18-20 12

GALATIANS

1:6 91
2:20 . 71, 72, 74-75, 78
2:21 38
5:24 .... 71, 77

EPHESIANS

3:6 86
3:16-19 146
5:22-33 .... 94, 95
5:25 94
5:26 94
5:28-29 94

PHILIPPIANS

1:23 113
3:10 .... 71, 72
3:12 ..... 78, 143-144

COLOSSIANS

1:9 19

I THESSALONIANS

2:7-8 122
5:3 142

I TIMOTHY

1:2 122
6:17 76

II TIMOTHY

1:2 122
1:3-4 122
1:5 122
3:2 75

TITUS

1:4 122
3:3 .... 35, 92

HEBREWS

1:3 132
2:10 .... 44-45, 81
11:19 51
13:11-13 150
13:12 .... 15, 150
13:13 120

I PETER

2:21 .... 71, 79
2:24 20,
   52, 64, 71, 79, 80
4:1 .... 77, 79, 83
4:1-2 80
4:13 .... 71, 72, 75

I JOHN

4:9 58
4:17 83
4:18 81

REVELATION

1:17-18 45
2:8 45
5:6 45
5:12 45
5:13 45
13:8 .... 45, 116
16:10-11 62